Born a Statistic

Living Rejected
Agreeing with
GOD

Shaneil "PJ" Yarbrough

Shaneil "PJ" Yarbrough

Self Publish 30 DAYS
This Is The Year For Your New Book

www.selfpublishn30days.com

Published by *Self Publish -N- 30 Days*

Copyright 2018 SY Revealed Ministries.

Printed in the United States of America

ISBN: 978-1724625434

1. Inspiration 2. Self Help

Shaneil Yarbrough: Revealed Ministries.

Born a Statistic

Disclaimer/Warning:

DEDICATION

This book is dedicated to my husband,
Larry D. Yarbrough, Sr., and our two sons,
Larry D. Yarbrough, Jr. (L.J.) and
Lance E. Yarbrough. Apart from life itself,
the three of you are my greatest blessings!

TABLE OF
CONTENTS

ENDORSEMENTS

"They won the victory over him because of the blood of the lamb and the word of their testimony. They didn't love their life so much that they refused to give it up." (Revelation 12:11, God's Word Translation).

In her first book, *"Born a Statistic, Living Rejected, Agreeing with God,"* Shaneil opens her life to the world giving her personal testimony. No matter where we have been or what we have done, there is hope for the hopeless and healing for the hurting. God has provided an example: Shaneil. During our eighteen years of marriage, I have personally witnessed Shaneil, with God's help, face her childhood pains, follow Christ's path and faithfully continue to proclaim God's goodness! She is my inspiration!

I know *"Born a Statistic, Living Rejected, Agreeing with God"* will touch you in the same way that Shaneil's life has touched mine. In closing, to ***My Mrs. America****:* I'm thankful God chose me to share life with you and our two amazing sons!

Larry D. Yarbrough, Sr., B.Th.
Changing Lives Ministries Church
El Dorado, AR

At the tender age of six, I met the author, Shaneil "PJ" Yarbrough. We were from "rival" towns, but that did not stop us from becoming friends. Our friendship has endured, and there has NEVER been an argument between the two of us. After all of these years, our bond is as strong as ever! We count this a blessing!

Funny enough, we quoted songs such as *"Jesus Keep Me Near the Cross," "Trouble Don't Last Always,"* and *"Weeping May Endure for a Night but Joy Comes in the Morning"* while in high school. However, it wasn't until we truly accepted Christ as the head of our lives that we actually knew the meaning of those lyrics!

BFF: you have a loving spirit and a HUGE heart for people!! To know you is to love you. Statistics say you should not be in the places or positions that you are in... but God! I am extremely proud of you and all of your accomplishments. I count it all joy to have you as my Best Friend Forever (BFF) for 34 years and counting. The best is yet to come!

Jamie Benton-Davis
El Dorado, AR

Oh, my!!! Reading this book "*Born a Statistic, Living Rejected, Agreeing with God*" by Author Shaneil Yarbrough reminds me of King David. The Bible says that David served God's purpose in his generation. That's what Shaneil is doing with this book! People in this hour desire the raw and honest God's truth, especially millennials. They need evidence of what God can bring them through with His mighty hand.

This book is a must-read and will give hope to a dying generation that they too can live in abundance and victory! Shaneil Yarbrough is truly serving her generation unapologetically and unashamedly. This is the Lord's doing; it is marvelous in our eyes!

Alphonso Montgomery, D. Div.
Led By the Spirit Church, Pastor
Little Rock, AR

This author's story is an essential read for everyone! I strongly encourage every woman regardless of your age, ethnic background, whether married, single, or divorced to read this book! Women struggling to overcome and silence the voices of guilt and shame from your past will be guided to a place of deliverance.

Shaneil Yarbrough, through her gifted skill to orate, shares her many triumphs in spite of the hardships of life. She is a perfect example of how with faith in God and determination to succeed, you may have been born a statistic but you can live in victory!

Monique F. Montgomery, Owner/Operator
Transformation Christian Beauty Salon
Little Rock, AR

I have been begging the author, Shaneil "PJ" Yarbrough, for years to share this story! Over our nearly 17 year friendship, she has shared tidbits here and there and I KNEW her story of overcoming was like none other. I am constantly amazed by PJ's sheer will and determination to NOT be a statistic and to PROVE that a perpetual cycle of poverty CAN cease to exist. As I read Born a Statistic (in less than one day), I found myself weeping over and over out of both devastation and immeasurable awe and joy. This book is the secret sauce EVERYONE born a statistic needs to read. Her dynamic story of struggle, perseverance and victory proves the chains of labels and circumstances can be broken!

Sara McDaniel, BSE, MSE
SimplySara.com
SimplySouthernCottage.com

Shaneil "PJ" Yarbrough's words fill me with compassion as they remind me that we can know very little about someone by simply looking at them. As a Pediatrician with an interest in early childhood trauma and its effects on lifelong health (physical, mental, relational), I noted the way that this story confirms what science tells us. Stressful experiences early in life have long-lasting effects that sometimes seem insurmountable, but with even one person who is present in the life of a child to give them love, hope and security, overwhelming odds don't have the final say.

Also, as a physician who believes in the power of the love of God, I again noted that PJ's words confirmed what science is now able to show us clearly. Brain and neural pathways set in place as responses to stress, trauma and abuse very early in life, can in fact be changed by the power of belief in God who created and loves us. Our minds are, quite literally, changed by faith. The author's personal determination, intentional gratitude and her choices to continue to choose to trust others and God's presence in her life, despite every reason not to, are truly inspiring. I know her words will bring hope and courage to many who may connect with her life's story and to those who may be in positions to be the ones who are that safe presence in the life of a child. I highly recommend this brave and inspiring story!

Dawn Muench, MD
Pediatrician
MA, Spiritual Formation and Leadership

CHAPTER 1

Born a Statistic

*"To whom then will ye liken me, or shall I be equal?
saith the Holy One. Lift up your eyes on high,
and behold who hath created these things, that
bringeth out their host by **number**: he calleth them
all by names by the greatness of his might, for
that he is strong in power; not one faileth."*

– Isaiah 40: 25, 26a (KJV)

Through the years, I have noticed that the word statistic is one that can be difficult to pronounce. Additionally, being that it is a mathematical term, the average person more than likely is not familiar with the depths and heights of the collection, classification, analysis, and interpretation of numerical facts or data [as defined in Merriam-Webster, Inc.] Statistics are most commonly applied in professions dealing with money and economics (i.e., engineering, science, education, biology, and sports). No worries, this book is not holistically about statistical concepts. Math is not my strong suit. As a matter of fact, I will probably say, "I'm not good with numbers," on a weekly basis. Because of that reality, I knew God gave me "Born a Statistic," as a part of this book's title.

When I began teaching fifth grade in the early 2000s, elementary teachers were responsible for teaching all subjects. Though math was my least favorite subject to teach, I always told my students that numbers were very important. To help them remember the order of operations, I used the famous acronym, PEMDAS, also known as the familiar phrase: "Please excuse my dear Aunt Sally" (which translates to parentheses, exponents, multiplication, division, addition, and subtraction).

With fake money, printed on green paper, I offered the experience of making purchases from our classroom store. Students displaying good behavior were allowed to "shop" on Fridays. I was the owner, manager, and cashier as they bought pencils, erasers, bookmarks, "no homework" passes, free recess tickets, etc. Due to the struggle I had experienced in my younger years with math, there were no limits when it came to educating young minds about numbers.

While I did not receive a solid, sure foundation in math-related theories and I sometimes still shy away from them as an adult, numbers are essential to life. In a sense, we [people] are often identified as numbers. How many times have you been asked to provide your Date of Birth, Social Security Number, Driver's License number, Student ID number, or Employee ID number? Countless times, right? Inmates are identified by a number. When people call your home or mobile device, they do that by dialing a number.

No matter how hard you try, one cannot escape numbers. I personally discovered this reality several years ago while attending a strategic planning meeting. A strategic planning meeting is a process by which an organization defines a strategy, makes decisions, or determines the direction in achieving a course of action. My first time in a setting such as this, I had an epiphany: I am a number, a statistic. A living, breathing statistic.

The strategic planning participants were divided into small focus groups and given specific topics to brainstorm. The emphasis for my group was "Children of Incarcerated Parents," and we were to determine ways to support children and families who were currently living out those unfortunate circumstances. I recall the discussion in my group beginning quite shallow, but it quickly ventured into deep waters.

Some people were quiet while others offered heartfelt comments. Since this was my first time attending, I was working hard at being seen – not heard. I'm known for being a little opinionated. Nonetheless, it wasn't long before I found myself jarred at the core to hear an accomplished, educated individual say, "Why does **THAT** have to be our focus? Most children whose parents are incarcerated will only follow in their footsteps." I could detect both the negativity and disdain in this gentleman's voice.

His demeanor was one of disgust, and his facial expression seemed to speak volumes. It took everything in me not to scream! All of a sudden, I felt very hot – physically and literally. My ears became warm (not a good sign) and I'm certain the expression on my face was telling. He had stirred up my "righteous indignation." I was beyond annoyed; therefore, it took some effort to remain professional. I decided to seize the moment. This encounter became one of the first times in my career that I had both the opportunity and ultimately the right to take a stand.

In that instant, passion partnered with purpose and I knew I had to speak up.

He had no idea, at that very moment, he was sitting next to a young lady whose mother *was* incarcerated. Actually, she had been the majority of my life. In that instant, passion partnered with purpose and I knew I had to speak up. In a strong yet slightly shaky voice, I began speaking before I knew it, "Excuse me, with all due respect, I must disagree. My birth mother is currently incarcerated, and she has been for most of my life. And although I've made my share of mistakes, I've never been arrested." I went on to say, "You see, like the children we are here to help, I was ***born a statistic*....**"

For years, I had known this, however, at that moment, I owned it. At first, I felt shame and regretted speaking up. As a matter of fact, I wanted to crawl under the table, but the secret was out. Up until that moment, my colleagues only knew me as an always bubbly, hardworking person.

Finally, I had mustered up the nerve to let the cat out of the bag – to expose my true self. Without any doubt, I know that attending that meeting was a pivotal moment in my life. There I was, an accomplished career woman, in a supervising role, yet vulnerable. As the man slowly sat back in his chair and others seemed to sit up at attention, there were some things I could have said, however, I said enough. They had no idea there was much more to my story.

Actually, I should rephrase that because my story is really HIStory! Like the introductory scripture of this chapter states, "He brings out their host by ***number*.**" This text references God drawing out troops and companies of His army. He has specific knowledge of them, calling each person by name. He makes use of them. He calls them to service, to what He has appointed. When I think of all I will share in this book, I find these words to be a great comfort.

> **The very things that might identify us as statistics can be the fuel that is needed to start a fire and ignite our passion to live life with purpose.**

I realize that I was born a statistic, but I do not have to remain one. Some will read "born a statistic" and immediately deem that a negative statement. But think of Jesus, the Savior of the world. Have you ever considered that Jesus was born a statistic? He was born to a teenage virgin (Mary) and was reared by a man (Joseph) who was not his biological father. Nonetheless, He is the only One whose number was called to save us from our sins.

God used Him, He became the ultimate servant, and only He could have been appointed to die on the cross! In the same way, I believe God has an exclusive plan for my life and yours. Each of us has a God-appointed "number." We have a precise assignment in the Kingdom of God. The very things that might identify us as statistics can be the fuel that is needed to start a fire and ignite our passion to live life with purpose. Straightforwardly, hardly a day goes by that I don't shake my head, pinch myself, or just look up towards Heaven and say, "Thank You, Lord!" With His help, I've defied the odds. Again, I'm the first to admit that I'm not good with numbers, but I do know without a shadow of a doubt that I was ***born a statistic***.

CHAPTER 2

The Early Years

*"Before I formed you in the womb,
I knew you. Before you were born, I set you apart
for my holy purpose..."*

– Jeremiah 1:5a (God's Word Translation)

Typically, when I share with people about my early years (ages 2–6), they quickly ask if I really remember. The answer is yes. Experiencing trauma at an early age can cause things to be imprinted on the brain. That said, I have an excellent memory which is sometimes both a blessing and curse. I remember a great deal from my early years, however, there are portions I can't recall. Maybe it's a good thing I can't dredge up all of the particulars. Speaking of details, I have asked, more than once. In fact, while in the process of writing this book, I asked my biological mother, Marsheill Finley (my biological father, Charley Roy Nichols, had passed), a series of questions in an effort to give her an opportunity to give her side of the story and to help me better understand my beginning.

She agreed to write down my questions, but I never received her responses. Questions that I thought were simple were obviously too complicated for her. Before my biological father passed away, I sat with him on a few occasions and asked him for some facts, but didn't get too far. Consequently, I have limited knowledge of what led to me being born which will be shared in the latter part of the book. The information I'm sharing is a combination of bits and pieces from my biological parents, adoptive parents, other family members, and one of my most prized possessions, my Adoption Summary. The summary is approximately one-hundred pages and has intrigued me from the moment I realized it existed (around age 10).

I'll never forget discovering this large roll of papers while "proging" (defined by the Urban dictionary as looking through a person's things without their knowledge or permission) in my adoptive parent's closet one day. While playing dress up and looking for the perfect outfit, I found this treasure. This document is a very comprehensive look into my early years; specifically birth – 6 years old. While most people can look through their baby memory book, this summary is my only record. That's right; unfortunately, I don't have any baby pictures. The only photo attached to the front of the Adoption Summary, captures me as a five-year-old. Those who know me can attest to (especially my two sons) how much I love photos and how often I can be caught with a camera in my hand - this explains why.

Thanks to medical documents included in the summary, I have knowledge of being born on September 9, 1978, weighing 6 pounds, 6.4 ounces. Due to raspy breathing, I was immediately placed in an incubator and observed for a few days before being discharged to my mother. I was born the third child of a teenage mother. Talk about a statistic! I once read that 3 out of 10 girls get pregnant before age 20. If my math is correct, that's nearly 750,000 teen pregnancies per year.

Each time I hear the phrase "babies having babies," I think of my biological mother. I had my first child in my early twenties, and it is extremely difficult for me to fathom having a child at age 16, 17, and then again at 18. At those ages, most girls are finishing high school and entering college. However, her experience was much different. In the summary, she reported that she completed ninth grade.

At the age of 19, she returned to school and attended the tenth grade, but dropped out a little over a month later. It goes on to say that her mother passed away at the age of 50 from a heart attack and she did not have a relationship with her father. These unfortunate circumstances led to her living with relatives (a large family with a full house) which resulted in the lack of parental guidance. Regrettably, the absence of nurturing, protective, and affectionate parents can be detrimental. The reality is that she was both a fatherless and motherless daughter. Under the Summary of my biological parents, this description is given for my mother:

"This child's mother is a small built Negro female, who lists herself as 5'6" tall, with a normal weight of approximately 120 pounds. She has short, curly black hair which she usually wears in an Afro. Her eyes are dark brown, her skin light brown, and has a round shaped face. She is attractive, well built with a well-proportioned figure. She is suspicious and distrustful of others, has difficulty holding a job, rarely shows warmth or affection, and is impulsive."

It took me years to see my mother from a perspective of grace. I realize now that her circumstances were not fully her fault, and I believe that her many deficiencies resulted in my sisters and I being born.

We came quickly, three consecutive years with a fourth girl being born four years after me. All four of us have different fathers. While I was very angry for many years and blamed her for everything, it is apparent that my mother was also born a statistic.

While I was very angry for many years and blamed her for everything, it is apparent that my mother was also born a statistic.

As for my biological father, he was nine years older than my mother. After serving in the Navy, during the Vietnam War, he returned to their small hometown of Russellville, Arkansas. This was approximately six years before my birth. They were friends which somehow eventually led to me a little later down the road. Interestingly enough, it's unclear whether or not he or she was aware that I was his child. Why do I say that? The summary states the following:

"This child's father is described as a black male, approximately 31 years of age 5'8" to 6'2" tall, and weighing 150 to 175 pounds. He has dark brown hair and black eyes. No other information is known. (The mother was unable to actually identify the father. The above is an approximation). This alleged father reportedly draws SSI benefits based on a disability. No other information is known. This alleged father is reported to have completed the 12th grade."

Though that information is brief and leaves a lot

to the imagination, thankfully, I was afforded the chance to meet and get to know my father. Later, I will reveal more.

Referring back to the Summary, medical records show that my mother admitted to drinking alcohol and smoking cigarettes throughout her pregnancy. She also received no prenatal care. I certainly don't have to explain how that could have ended in me being a statistic.

Evidenced by detailed doctor's notes, I had 6 hospital stays. This was a total of approximately 35 days before my second birthday. Pages and pages of these notes indicate that during my first year of life, I was diagnosed with "Failure to Thrive" (FTT). Statistically, FTT is found in 5 to 10 percent of children in the United States and can result in death. Failure to Thrive is most commonly a sign of under-nutrition. Families with children suffering from this usually have other factors including mental health disorders, inadequate nutritional knowledge, and financial difficulties – poverty. In fact, Stedman's Medical Dictionary states that poverty is the greatest single risk factor of FTT. One page of the doctor's notes reads as follows:

"The baby [Shaneil] was admitted here for the second time to the Hospital, and the baby is now 7

months old, black female, who has failure to thrive. She was admitted when she was 2 months old and found to gain weight after she had been losing weight at home. She was not brought back in for her follow up, and she is still extremely small, her weight and height being below the three-standard deviations. After admission, she took 14 ounces of formula. She proceeded to gain weight rapidly, here in the hospital, over the next three days that she was here. She gained 9 ounces, so apparently it is just inadequate feeding at home. Child Protective Services have been contacted, and this case should be followed closely with weekly intervals in the clinic to ensure that the baby continues to gain weight."

The next account, one month later, states that, "The baby has lost weight over the preceding two to three weeks..." In the first 24 months of my life, my medical issues included: chronic bronchial asthma, chickenpox, multiple colds and the flu, inadequate weight gain, herpetic stomatitis (ulcers in the

Image of me attached to the Adoption Summary (1983)

mouth), various viruses, conjunctivitis (pink eye), boils on my scalp, and a mysterious burn to the right leg. I have memories of being in a crib with thick white bars looking up at a nurse or doctor looking down at me. I was very young; nevertheless, the recollections of bright lights and the cold atmosphere are striking. While the average infant gains an average of 2 pounds per month, with the above mentioned medical history, it is a little easier to understand why I barely reached 20 pounds a month after my 2nd birthday.

To realize how close you were to death (at such an early age) is an eye-opening experience. Psalm 23:4 says, *"Even though I walk through the valley of the shadow of the death, I will fear no evil, for you are with me..."* Obviously, I was too young to comprehend the seriousness of these events, however, I am eternally grateful that God was there the entire time. As I read my medical history, I can trace His hand, literally preserving my life! Though I was innocent and helpless, He was faithful to watch over me.

For years, I would pull out the Adoption Summary and have a big pity party. My thoughts were, "Poor me. I was such an ill child. My mother didn't take care of me. I almost died." No wonder I hate doctors and medicine! Why did God let me suffer like that? How did I make it? These days, as I read the medical transcripts, I am overcome by a wellspring of emotions; predominantly gratitude!

Because of God's love, His healing virtue, and His matchless power, the enemy was defeated!

I understand that Satan desired to kill me. He knew what God had planned for my life. Satan took a glimpse into my future, and he wanted to end my life. Because of God's love, His healing virtue, and His matchless power, the enemy was defeated! In fact, God strategically put the right people in my path – some medical professionals who were observant enough to see harmful patterns.

Moreover, the vast number of medical emergencies led to the Department of Human Services becoming involved (referred to as CPS – Child Protective Services in the document).

CHAPTER 3

The Apartment – Home (Not So) Sweet Home

"And my people shall dwell in a peaceable habitation, and in sure dwellings, and in quiet places..."

– Isaiah 32:18 (KJV)

Records reflected that my mother was "re-assigned" a Child Protective Service (CPS) caseworker in 1978 (court documents show that there was a previously opened case for my 1 and 2 year old sisters). A course of action was put in place which called for frequent follow-up visits. It didn't take long for the doctor's findings and the case worker's notes to begin overlapping, building suspiciousness of neglect and/or abuse. After multiple visits and threats to take us away because of failure to comply, my second birthday brought about a significant occurrence.

I was officially taken into the custody of CPS for the first time. This resulted in yet another hospital stay and placement in a foster home. This particular removal was temporary. The Summary reveals that my sisters and I were taken into custody several more times (overnight or for several days). A total of 212 days are documented as "days of placement." I don't remember each place or the people, but I do recall the emotions that I developed because of the frequent disruptions.

In my former work as an Early Childhood Consultant, I facilitated workshops which encouraged participants to reflect on their childhood. I did this to supply the catalyst they needed to provide children with rich experiences. Countless times I asked these professionals to share their earliest childhood memory. As they began to share happy, funny, or pleasant memories, without fail, the same disturbing images would surface for me.

In my mind's eye, I can see myself standing at the entrance of a small apartment. I can see the living area and kitchen combined with very little furniture. There are three more small rooms, two bedrooms with a bathroom nestled between them. The apartment smells of burning incense, cigarette smoke, beer, and other alcoholic beverages. I was later informed that this small apartment was actually in the "projects;" government-funded housing. Unlike the scripture referenced from Isaiah 32:18, this was not a place of peace. It was not quiet or a secure dwelling.

In fact, I only have two good memories from that apartment: (1) being in the bathtub with my sisters, giggling and splashing water (2) running and riding some type of wheeled toy up and down a steep slope or hill. When those memories pass through my mind,

I can recall the laughter of my sisters and myself – we seemed happy. Regrettably, the bad outweighs the good when it comes to my other remembrances from that residence. The other strolls down memory lane include less joyous events.

The Feeding America website reveals that 1 in 5 children face hunger and approximately 16 million go to bed hungry every night. That is an alarming statistic and one with which I can relate. Once they were aware, many of my friends and associates were anxious to hear my story about why I decided not to eat chicken until the end of 2010 (at age 32). In essence, it's simple. I recall many red, white, and blue Kentucky Fried Chicken buckets in our quaint, little apartment. The unappetizing factor is that most of the time, the buckets were filled with the leftover bones.

After my mother and her friends would finish enjoying their meal, my siblings and I were left to fend for ourselves. I recall eating from chicken bones (with very little meat remaining), consuming raw spaghetti and raw potatoes. Even now, it's difficult for me to imagine myself gnawing on bones for nourishment. There was no excuse for that. Obviously I don't know for sure, but I think a young mother with three young girls was receiving some type of assistance. Having the basic need of food unmet has stayed with me. Years later, I was told that I referred to chicken as "Funky Fried Chicken!" I eventually overcame my refusal to eat chicken. It was brought to my attention that my unforgiveness was the issue, not the chicken. Thankfully, I worked through it and learned to forgive, but honestly, fried chicken still isn't on my list of favorite foods!

Another incident involves a truth that many people; young and old struggle to both share and conquer. Beginning at a very young age (3 or 4), I was sexually violated numerous times. No matter what the source, child sexual abuse statistics are staggering. Sadly, experts agree that occurrences are far greater than what is actually reported. That truth is both disturbing and heartbreaking. Needless to say, telling the world that I am one of the millions is not an easy task. My prayer is that someone hearing my story will rise above what has happened to them. Most times, I spare my audience the details because more times than not, I'm speaking to a group of people who frankly can't handle it. In this book, I finally have a platform to bear all and tell my truth. Doing this is not easy, but it's necessary.

Put bluntly, my small, fragile body was raped by a very large, adult male. He would always start by taking off all of my clothes. After that, he would pinch my nipples and slap my buttocks. On a small couch, in that apartment, he would smother me by climbing on top of me, kissing me hard in the mouth, and touching me inappropriately between my legs. The pain of him thrusting against me is something that I've had to cast out of my mind for years. To add to this heinous activity, he would make me do things to him as well.

Each time I recall these acts, there is an ache in the pit of my stomach. Much later in life, I discovered that this was a mentally ill neighbor (potentially an extended family member) who would "babysit" for my mother while she was "out."

Over 30 years later, I came face to face with him and recognized his voice immediately. He beckoned for me, "Hey, cuz, hey cuz (short for cousin), I need to talk to you!" In that moment, the emotions began to overflow, and without any effort, I knew who he was. Thankfully, I was among close family and friends and found comfort in them.

Fending for ourselves, in the absence of a consistent caregiver, we were left many times with the potential of the worst happening. As I think of all of the things that could have transpired, I know, with a shadow of a doubt, that angels were encamped around us. Only God knows how many meals we missed, the times we were in danger and the tragedies that we barely escaped.

> **Only God knows how many meals we missed, the times we were in danger and the tragedies that we barely escaped.**

Currently, one of my daily prayers is that God should protect my family and me from dangers seen and unseen. Clearly, He has been doing that for a myriad of years! In this home (not so) sweet home, I experienced one of the most traumatic transitions in my lifetime. That day, with no warning, strange people entered the apartment. There was a lot of silence in the atmosphere that day; however, it's such a loud memory.

Our clothes were thrown into laundry baskets and black garbage bags; we were picked up by a very tall Caucasian gentleman (for years, I thought he was a giant), rushed out the door and put into the backseat of a vehicle. Except in my mind, I never saw that place again. The feelings of confusion that seemed to be overtaking my young mind, combined with the blank stare and sealed lips of my mother sitting on the couch, are forever engraved in my mind. That was September 8, 1982, the day before my fourth birthday. This time, when CPS took us into their custody, it was permanent:

"The child [Shaneil] and her siblings (2 girls) entered foster care after the mother's failure to carry through a series of orders by the court which were intended to safeguard the children's welfare. Social Services worked with the family since 1976, and the mother failed to cooperate with their workers and continued chronic neglect of the children, particularly leaving the children without supervision of care for extended periods of time."

To this point, everything I've shared happened from birth to 4 years of age. Articles, books, and studies that I've read say that statistically, as a young child who was abandoned, neglected, rejected, abused, and orphaned, I was likely to end up a misfit; a cold, cruel, abusive, horrible person.

In fact, I had every right and reason to live my life as a person with a chip on my shoulder, displaying a "woe is me" attitude, and refusing to see the bright side of things. Surely, no one would have blamed me. Lack and dysfunction were all I knew. Fortunately, God had a different plan. From the time I was conceived in my mother's womb, He knew me, and He had a purpose for me [and my many struggles]. The circumstances that I've talked about were all out of my control, but God was always in control. One might argue that He was being a harsh God, but on the contrary, He was being merciful. I've learned to look at life from a Godly perspective.

> **With God's help, I have a testimony instead of tears, and I give praise to God instead of looking for pity.**

As you continue reading, you will learn that I love acronyms. One that I created was based on how I lived for too many years, as a **V.I.C.T.I.M. V**iciously, **I**mposing, **C**unning, **T**raits to **I**mpress and/or, **M**anipulate – all in order to seek out sympathy. No more! With God's help, I have a testimony instead of tears, and I give praise to God instead of looking for pity. He turned all of my oppositions into opportunities! Speaking of opportunities, I'd like to paraphrase one of my favorite scriptures, 2 Corinthians 12:9, God looks for opportunities to show His mercifulness in our lives. And He promises that His grace is sufficient for every affliction. With that thought in mind, I decided a long time ago that He found many opportunities to show mercy on me and when I was most afflicted, His grace remained intact!

> **God's grace has allowed Satan's plan to be interrupted and many strongholds have been broken.**

God's grace has allowed Satan's plan to be interrupted and many strongholds have been broken. In spite of what I've endured, a new path has been set for my children and my children's children to continue in a different, better way.

With the uncertainty of my first few years of life and only a roll of tattered court documents (my Adoption Summary) as a roadmap to the beginning of this journey called life, I'm sure you're curious about what happened next.

When I allowed my dear friend, Sara, to read what you've read so far, she replied with some questions:

- Where did that man take you?

- Did you ever see your mom again?

- What about your biological father?

- How was your development as a child and student?

- What happened to your sisters?

- How did you overcome all of the labels that had been placed on you?

- What's the "secret sauce" to how and why you've made it and are able to write this book?

I promise to answer all of these questions as you continue reading.

CHAPTER 4

Do You Promise to Keep Me?

"The Lord is not slow in keeping His promise..."

— 2 Peter 3:9a

The Department of Human Services (DHS) office was, unfortunately, a familiar place. There were lots of toys to play with, nice people, and I remember feeling a sense of security. I'm sure behind the scenes, the caseworkers were frantically trying to find placements for children. As official wards of the state, documentation speaks of times when I slept on the floor of the office, went home with employees, and I even spent time in a couple of group home settings. The places where I stayed were not always pleasant.

Notes from a survey conducted of one placement revealed that I complained of not being fed when hungry. Another foster family reported that I cried too much and wanted to be babied. Imagine that! A child who had recently been ripped from everything that was familiar and comfortable cried too much. Forgive my sarcasm. One lady (not sure of her role) was questioned about multiple bruises and scratches that she said were from "rough play."

The caseworker's opinion stated that *"Shaneil is an active, happy child, but has never shown signs of being rough. Other options for placement are being explored."*

It seems that some of these places were a long commute from the Russellville area. Unfortunately, foster homes in the early 1980's were not in abundance. Even now, where I live (Union County, Arkansas) and all over the world, homes for displaced children are few. By chance, about 15 miles from Russellville, in Atkins, there were two homes with room for my two sisters and me.

I remember riding in the car along a winding road. The trees looked like skyscrapers. Two elderly ladies (they were sisters) and their husbands lived a few minutes down the road from one another. Both couples were foster parents. There was only one problem. Neither of the couples was willing to take all three of us. Statistically speaking, sibling groups are often separated while in the foster care system. The majority of separations occur during foster home placement and reunification is rare.

In our case, I was placed alone, and my two older sisters were placed together. Since we were literally down the road from one another, we had frequent contact. We visited often, played together, attended the same church and rode the bus to school together. Oddly, sometimes when I think back on these days, I realize that my young mind could not fully understand what was taking place. The new environment, strange people and their way of life were confusing.

As a matter of fact, I don't believe I always realized my sisters were my sisters. Being with them for short periods of time and then having to leave them was always difficult. Regrettably, I learned the sting of separation anxiety during this process. I can remember crying profusely because I didn't understand why we couldn't be together. Even though this was very difficult, there are some positive things that I remember from this foster placement.

This home is where I can remember attending church. It was a small, older building with a pianist frequently playing the song, "One Day at a Time (Sweet Jesus)." I can still hear the congregation singing and now appreciate how it was a great representation of that time in my life. My foster parents were an elderly African American couple. I called them "Mom and Poppa." Although they were up in age, they lived an active life.

Their days were filled with gardening, cooking, raising chickens, and rearing their young granddaughter, my playmate. A tiny, red rocking chair was my favorite place to sit in a small den/playroom in the rear of the house. My playmate and I would play dolls; I would pretend to be the teacher and "read books" for my first student. I loved to comb her hair. Speaking of hair, my foster mom's extremely long mane was absolutely beautiful! It was so long that she would place her hair on the ironing board to brush out the kinks. Isn't it amazing what we remember?

Also, my foster mom's smile seemed to light up the room. She frequently gave me tight hugs and always kissed me on my forehead. Outside the home was red clay dirt. Once, I dug a huge hole as deep as I could because my childish mind was sure that the devil lived underneath! Thank goodness I was wrong! Lastly, I fell in love with hot dogs and sauerkraut while in their care. Even now, the smell of it brings up the many times I ate from an aluminum pie pan. I wish I could say every day in this home was pleasurable; however, that was not the case.

There are definitely other foods like sardines, potted meat, and saltine crackers that I'd rather not eat because they were served so often. When I was a "bad girl," these items were my breakfast, lunch, and dinner. No matter how many times I said I didn't like those foods, I was forced to eat them. Additionally, although I had already experienced a lot before entering that home, it was there that the root Spirit of Fear crept into my life. 2 Timothy 1:7 says, *"For God hath not given us the spirit of fear, but of power, and of love, and of a sound mind."*

After reading Dr. Henry Malone's *Shadow Boxing*, I was able to identify this root spirit and how it has operated in my life through the fruit of fright, nightmares, **nyctophobia** (fear of the dark), cynophobia (fear of dogs), worry, anxiety, and paranoia. I think a degree of the fear related to darkness is common to child development. In my case, fright, nightmares, and nyctophobia originated in the bedroom of this foster home. After being put to bed each night, the lights were turned off and the clutter that was somehow invisible during the day seemed to come to life around me.

Clothing, linens, and miscellaneous items were stacked up all around the room. The bedroom closet was so full that it remained open at all times with items seeping out. In my childhood imagination, these harmless, lifeless objects appeared to transform into creatures, goblins, monsters, and the "Bogeyman." You know the Bogeyman, right? He was the one used to scare children into good behavior.

Isn't it interesting how Satan strategically takes an innocent thing and turns it into something else? Those fears followed me for years. No matter where I went, the shadows were there. I'm certain this is where my strong need for things to be in order started. Everything has a specific place. My preference is to have all clothes and items put away and my closet door shut before going to bed. As a matter of fact, I often joke that I don't have obsessive-compulsive disorder (OCD) but instead CDO because that would be the disorder's name in "ABC" order.

Atkins is also where my apprehension of dogs also originated. While many children are fascinated with animals, (for example our youngest son, Lance) but I was not. Over time, I've decided that several factors led to my uneasiness. Firstly, I don't recollect being exposed to animals before living in this home. Hearing the dogs bark, particularly at me, was new and unfamiliar. Additionally, I was not eased into having pets. In fact, I was literally thrust into this environment. Every morning, after I was served my oatmeal and juice, I was told to "go outside and play."

Remember? My foster parent's hobbies included several outdoor activities. Staying in the house to watch television was forbidden. For that reason, I was outdoors the greater part of the day, terrorized. Many people say that dogs can smell or sense your fear and I believe it. It seemed the dogs would be occupied until I was in their space and then the bullying would begin.

My foster dad would scold the animals, but it wasn't long before they would start snarling, growling, and barking. Their fierceness would force me to the top of the steps where I sat until I was allowed to re-enter the house. Unfortunately, after going in for lunch or at the end of the day, I still couldn't escape the dogs. The first several minutes on the inside were spent removing large, dog ticks from both my legs and arms. This removal process required a cautious and thorough method with tweezers. It was very painful and disgusting too! As a result, my legs were badly scarred from this daily routine. I will never understand why I couldn't stay in the house. Nevertheless, that explains the beginning of the cynophobia.

The fruit of worry, anxiety, and paranoia entered via a different avenue and ultimately grew into the Spirit of Heaviness. I refer to it as "the beginning of my end;" rejection. Do you ever argue with yourself? I do.

An argument that I can't seem to settle with myself is who the first person to reject me was. I go back and forth with myself about whether my biological mother or my foster mother was the beginning to my end. I previously stated that my biological mother was silent as we were removed from the apartment. Unfortunately, that is my only memory of her from my young years. However, I vividly remember this short but monumental conversation that I randomly had with my foster mother:

Me: Am I a good girl?

Foster Mother: Yes, you are a good girl.

Me: Do YOU promise to keep me?

Foster Mother: Yes, baby, we are going to keep you. This is your home.

One part of me wants to believe that those were her intentions, but the overwhelming feeling is that she only said what she knew I wanted/needed to hear. In that small encounter, the seed of rejection that my mother and father inaudibly dropped was now watered. While it is many times downplayed, rejection is real. This statement may seem contradictory, but my experience is that nothing carries you as far as rejection yet takes

This statement may seem contradictory, but my experience is that nothing carries you as far as rejection yet takes you nowhere.

you nowhere. The emotions that are associated with rejection cannot be ignored. The intensity of the pain is much like the scale that doctors and nurses use when they ask patients their pain level. In my opinion, when it comes to rejection, it's always a 10 or above! That's why I say this was the "beginning of my end." You may ask, the end to what?

Honestly, this seed of rejection was the end to countless things. Some are easy to articulate, and there are others that there aren't sufficient words to describe. As you read more, you will better understand the second portion of the title "Living Rejected."

Before I re-visit the conversation that I had with my foster mother, this is a good time to mention that shortly after entering this foster home, my third sister was born. My mom was now 23 and the mother of four girls. Soon after giving birth, my youngest sister was also taken into custody. Her foster care placement was also separate from my sisters and me. Consequently, the four of us were in three different locations. We saw her during visits at DHS, but those memories are very hazy. Statistically speaking, four biological siblings, in three different homes would surely not end well.

"We are going to keep you," are words that will be forever entrenched in my memory. In the Adoption Summary, a section entitled: "Preparation of the Child for Adoption" discloses other discussions that relate to this subject matter.

The preparation of the children for adoption was initiated in March, 1983, with discussions with the children about the various reasons they had come into foster care, why they had to stay in foster care, and why a return to their mother did not seem too feasible. At this time, Shaneil cried. Her foster parents followed up and gave feedback of her lack of understanding and acceptance. Her foster parents discussed the possibility of adopting her, but did not want any of the three sisters and decided it would be best if the four of them could be adopted together. Her foster mother reported that Shaneil said, "You promised to keep me."

Undoubtedly, at four and half years old, I was like any other young child who had been told something by a trusted adult. Regardless of the reality I was facing, like a child anticipating Christmas morning, I had high hopes of receiving everything I wanted.

When my foster mother uttered those words, I took them to heart and expected that outcome. And although I believe her intentions were well, the promise was broken. When I think of my strong sense of skepticism, it's fairly easy to trace it back to these moments.

In the absence of my parents, my foster parents were the people I trusted most. They fed me, clothed me, cared for me when I was ill and comforted me when I was scared. However, when this life-changing decision presented itself, in my eyes, I was failed. This helps me to understand my tendencies to be suspicious of people and their true intent. Take my word for it; there is a reason people are the way they are.

As I write, I cannot help but ponder how many doors I failed to walk through, the relationships I sabotaged, and more

As I write, I cannot help, but ponder how many doors I failed to walk through, the relationships I sabotaged, and more importantly, the opportunities I forfeited to be used by God.

importantly, the opportunities I forfeited to be used by God. I can now admit that I have the propensity to be leery of people. When it was first brought to my attention, I denied it. I'm now cognizant of my reluctance to trust and how I rarely allow individuals to get close to me.

It was only after I learned that only God is capable of keeping all of His promises that I was challenged to do things differently. God is not slow to keep His promises. Once we comprehend that fact, we can let down our guards and trust Him to do the rest. Psalm 118:8 states, *"It is better to trust in the Lord than to put confidence in man."*

I have learned that when I fully depend on God (in all areas of my life), He gives instructions, guides my steps, and even takes on the task of safeguarding my heart.

CHAPTER 5

All or None

*"Behold, I am the Lord, the God of all flesh;
is there anything too hard for me?"*

— *Jeremiah 32:27*

One of the most interesting parts of the Adoption Summary is entitled "Recommendations." This section proposes the recommendations for adoption. The first paragraph gives an overview of the suggestions made by the Department of Human Services staff:

"The ideal placement would be for all four children to be placed together in a black adoptive home with an adoptive mother and father aged 27 to 31, and adequate financial means to support the four of them. This potential adoptive family would need to be versatile as each of these children are different with different strengths and needs."

Following that, the document continues with a great deal of detail offering an in-depth description of me. The report is a combination of notes from my case worker, foster mom, and my preschool (Head Start) teacher. It baffles me how these people (who were not related to me) knew me so well. Their words prove that they played an instrumental part in my life. They easily pinpointed both my personality and my overall demeanor. These notes, conspicuously about me (abbreviated below) are among those that I cherish and re-read often.

"Shaneil was nicknamed "Pinky" because her mother used to dress her in pink always. She is friendly, alert, and bright. She is talkative and trusting. Her teacher described her as "bossy," "observant," and a leader. She is a loving child with a lot of affection to give. She giggles a lot when she is happy or excited. She gets along with others and has a lot of friends. She has a sense of humor and enjoys doing things that are "fun." She is very easily disciplined, needing only a look, a tone of voice, or light verbal discipline. She had a good deal of self-control. She tries to "mother" other small children. She needs a family who will appreciate her ability to self-discipline. She needs a family who will emphasize achievement in school, challenge and motivate her, and stimulate her intelligence and academic potential."

There are many reasons why I value these words so much. I no longer use the nickname "Pinky," but pink is (and always will be) my favorite color. My biological mother definitely got that right. Presently, only people who knew me as a toddler refer to me as "Pinky." It doesn't bother me, but it is always a reminder that they apparently have knowledge of my rocky beginning. I'm amazed each time I read this portion of the Adoption Summary. It outlines things about me as a four-year-old that are still relevant today.

My temperament, conduct, and the particulars about how I generally dealt with things at age 4 are almost verbatim to who I am as I quickly approach age 40! When I speak to Early Childhood professionals, I always encourage them to realize that they have the awesome responsibility of doing what my preschool teacher did; pay attention and be present! My mother was not around, and my foster mom was away from me many hours throughout the day. Nevertheless, my teacher was very intentional about getting to know me.

. . . .

My temperament, conduct, and the particulars about how I generally dealt with things at age 4 are almost verbatim to who I am as I quickly approach age 40!

. . . .

Her conscientious effort to provide the caseworker with annotations that would be useful [to potential adoptive parents] was the most detailed and accurate account available. I'm convinced that this was only possible through her dedication to going above teaching academics. She obviously invested time in establishing a relationship and capitalized on moments to get to know me on a personal level. I have no doubt that this teacher (who is unfortunately nameless) and my daily involvement in her classroom is directly related to the comfort I have always felt when attending school. I will say more about that later.

Following the narrative, several potential outcomes are listed in the Recommendations.

1. As previously mentioned, if at all possible, the four girls should all be adopted together.

2. Since Shaneil has been in foster care alone, she could easily be adopted alone.

3. The older two girls, Latosha and Latreace, have been in the same foster home and could be adopted together.

4. The baby girl, Ashley, has been in foster care alone and could be adopted alone.

5. Shaneil and the older girls (3 total) have had frequent contact (almost daily) and would benefit from being together.

6. The two younger girls could be adopted together.

7. The older girls could be adopted together.

8. One of the older girls and Shaneil could be adopted together.

9. One of the older girls and the baby girl could be adopted together.

10. All four girls could be adopted separately.

11. A combination of any two of the girls could be made based on dispositions that will best suit the children.

Even knowing the outcome, each time I read those eleven options, it appears hopeless! With these four young lives at stake, how would this ever work out? Before I answer that question, I have to admit that I regret never sitting down to ask more questions and fill in more blanks about exactly how this all transpired. At the same time, I love the fact that I'm unable to evoke all of the details because that allows me to appreciate better just how miraculous this part of my story is.

That leads me to introducing my readers to a couple in their mid-40s. They lived in a small, South Arkansas community (Calion) with merely four hundred people. Andrew Curley was a truck driver and his wife, Ernestine, was a saw operator at the local sawmill. They were well known in the area with a host of family and friends. They had been married for many years, but they did not have children together.

Image of sisters prior to adoption. (L to R) Ashley, Latosha, LaTreace, and Shaneil.

The story (as it was told to me) started with a commercial or some type of television advertisement that showcased a photograph of four little girls [us] who were in foster care and available for adoption. Obviously, things have changed a lot in 30 plus years because confidentiality requirements prohibit children in foster care from being identified publicly. In spite of this, from my understanding, she instantly fell in love and contacted the person identified as the case manager and inquired about my sisters and me.

After she shared her plans with a few close friends, they asked her if she was "crazy?" The most difficult hurdle came when she decided to share her heart's desire with her husband. I can only imagine the nervousness she felt to suggest that their child-less home goes from zero to four girls! I believe in my heart that she prayed about it and asked her friends to pray as well. When she finally did approach her husband, she said he was initially resistant to the idea.

I am sure in his mind this was an outlandish idea! When she would tell this story, she would laugh while saying that she told him if he did not go with her, she would pick out a drunken man, clean him up, dress him in a suit and have him sign the necessary paperwork. Well, I guess that got his attention! At some point, the pair, Andrew and Ernestine, made the six-hour round trip (on a few occasions) to visit and get to know us. Knowing the system, I'm sure all of the proceedings, visits, court dates, etc. took an extensive amount of time.

Yet my memory instantaneously skips to our adoption day celebration! I know that's weird, right? Unfortunately, that is how my brain (concerning my earlier years) is wired. I distinctly remember what could have very well been my first time in a restaurant. Everything was bright red inside the establishment. This may seem small and insignificant to some, but to me, it is so sentimental. We, the Curley family, ate our first family meal in a Pizza Hut. We were all dressed in shades of pink and red. I can recall shaking parmesan cheese on my pizza, sitting in my new Daddy's lap, and hugging my new Mama. It was a great day indeed!

As you can see, this courageous couple made the unpopular decision to make recommendation number one a reality! The "all or none" assertion made by our adoptive parents allowed us to have the opportunity to grow up as sisters and family. Our biological mother had lost any chance of getting us back. In spite of this, we had one another. This outcome was not only unexpected, but also virtually impossible. But with God, all things are possible. Nothing is too hard for Him.

....

The "all or none" assertion made by our adoptive parents allowed us to have the opportunity to grow up as sisters and family.

....

It goes without saying that we could have literally ended up in four different corners of the world. But God! His plan was bigger than the pain we had endured. The dilemma had blossomed into a divine appointment. As my life has introduced its ups and downs, I have always been able to revert to the late summer/fall of 1984.

After nearly five years of going in and out of the custody of the state, things were finally turning around. There is no doubt in my mind that my situation, which started out bleak, shifted because of God's mercy and love.

He was on my side, and He is on your side! Please don't allow circumstances to make you think any differently. What you are facing may seem unbearable and irreparable. I want to encourage you to trust God. He did the unimaginable for my sisters and me. And He's the same God yesterday, today, and forever more. Expect Him to do an "All or None" kind of miracle in your life!

CHAPTER 6

Everything New

"Behold I will do a new thing."

— Isaiah 43:19

I have turned to this familiar passage in Isaiah countless times. Most commonly, I visit this text when I am about to encounter something outside of my comfort zone. Some things are like a new, perfectly-fitted pair of high-heeled shoes. When that is the case, there's a sense of gratification and excitement.

On the other hand, some things do not come with such a feeling. In fact, it can be the complete opposite – absolutely unpleasant and terrifying. My prediction is that if a poll were done to determine who likes change, the majority of those being asked would not be in favor of it. Quite the reverse, I have never been resistant to change. I accredit that to my array of experiences from birth to six years old. As I just mentioned, I was only a few days past my sixth birthday; however, I plainly remember what it felt like to have everything new.

When I woke up from the three-hour car ride in our new car, my heart was racing [that happens a lot; even now, when I'm excited]! Located at 848

Gum St. was a big white house, our new home. Our new parents, who we quickly transitioned to calling "Mama and Daddy," led us inside while bringing in our belongings and explaining we were home. The quick tour revealed our new bedroom and our new living environment. The home was very neat. The family room contained a wood-burning stove, a couch, nice chairs, and a formal dining table.

The next room, the kitchen, had another table with four chairs, which would become where we ate our daily meals. The bedrooms were spacious, and there was a small den with a television. One bathroom was in the hallway along with one of my favorite things, a small set of shelves (a library) with a collection of books and a few sets of encyclopedias. I don't recall the specifics of our first few days there, but I do remember feeling good about being there. This was especially true because I was with all three of my sisters.

Within a short period, we were introduced to what I refer to as our "triangular lifestyle." Primarily, there were three aspects of this new adventure: meeting new family members, attending a new church, and enrolling in a new school. Actually, these three things essentially made up our new way of life. New family members included our grandparents. Our adoptive mother's mom and step-father, "Big Mama" and "Big Daddy" lived two hours away near Little Rock. We visited them on the weekends. Our adoptive father's mother lived less than a mile away. We also called her "Big Mama" and saw her almost daily.

We also met two new siblings, two brothers, (one each from our parent's first marriages). Mama did not give birth to either of them. As a matter of fact, she was diagnosed as barren. When we were much older, she explained that she had multiple miscarriages. Both brothers were already grown when we came along. One of them lived in the home (a few different times) when we were children. Other family members included a few close cousins and a handful of extended relatives.

Outside of our grandparents and a few cousins, we were never close to many of our family members. Perhaps it is a stretch of my imagination or I watch too much television, but I always envisioned a huge "WELCOME HOME" party to officially introduce us to our family. That never happened. In fact, while most people who adopt are surrounded by their families with excitement, support, and love, primarily, our parents were all we had. Even now, I am not close to anyone in my adoptive family.

The second aspect of our lives was our new church, Willow Grove Missionary Baptist Church. Many of the people who worshiped with us were basically an extension of our family. There were at least five or six women in the congregation who we called "Aunt." They were not biological sisters of our parents (my mother was an only child, and my father only had brothers), but close enough to our mother and family that the title became a term of endearment. These ladies were kind and supportive, specifically to my mom as she was taking on the new role of being a mother. She attended church on a more consistent basis than my dad and always made sure we were there.

Speaking of being there, I loved everything about the church. This may seem like an odd statement about me as a young girl, but when I attended church, I sensed that I had a purpose. Whether I was attending Sunday school, Baptist Training Union (BTU), youth meeting, choir rehearsal, or serving as a Jr. Usher, I was excitedly involved. I loved studying my Sunday school lessons, writing notes and preparing to do the review of the lesson in front of the congregation. On top of all of that, almost immediately, I became what some referred to as the "Pastor's Pet."

I'm sure you have heard the term "Teacher's Pet," and this relationship was virtually the same thing. While some couldn't understand why I was the child that was favored, hindsight is 20/20. My pastor, Dr. Pete Lambert, and his wife, Sister Ollie, saw something in me that I did not realize existed. I have thanked God many times for their invitations to attend additional church services. While we would travel, he would "test" me on Bible stories and tell me that God had "something very special for me to do."

Because of the seeds they sowed, I established knowledge of the Bible, a sure foundation in Christian living, and a personal love-filled relationship with God. Another reason I am thankful to have such God-sent spiritual leaders in my childhood is because their unconditional love always outweighed the hatred in church. A lot of people have experienced church hurt, and in my case, it began when I was a child.

Before our adoption, my mother was essentially a "community mother." She was the youth leader at church and had previously welcomed some young people into her home. Subsequently, after she brought us home, things changed. My sisters and I were unaware that we had become their competition. "Mean girls" is the best description for some of the girls my age and a little older who made a habit of treating me badly.

As much as I loved the feeling of doing what I thought was right [before God], I also dreaded the comments about how I needed to stop trying to be better than everyone. Having the spirit of rejection haunt me so early, I subsequently became a people-pleaser as far back as I can remember. As much as I knew being involved in the church was right, I was growing weary in my well doing and contemplated quitting multiple times!

The one thing that kept me grounded in the church was my love for music. One Thursday night at youth choir rehearsal, I "found" my voice. When there was an opportunity for a lead part, out of nowhere, I said, "I'll do it!" I didn't know if I knew I could sing, but I wanted to try.

When I opened my mouth, out came the words, "*One step, one step - all you have to do is take one step and He will do the rest.*" I'll never forget that moment. Though I wasn't aware of what that warm feeling was at the time, now, I certainly realize that the Spirit of God had filled my heart and mouth with a new song. From that point on, during nearly every church service, I sang.

Sometimes it was in the devotion period, *"Guide me, O Thou great Jehovah, pilgrim through this barren land."* Other times it was during the offering: *"God put a rainbow in the sky...it looked like the sun wasn't gon' shine anymore...God put a rainbow in the sky... oooo, ooo!"*

Countless times, I sang in the choir and on many occasions, at the end of a song, I would burst into tears. I felt so overwhelmed with emotions that I couldn't adequately express. My mom would send me to the water fountain with instructions to take three sips of water: "One for the Father, one for the Son, and one for the Holy Spirit."

Funny enough, it was enough to calm me down. As I grew older and was exposed to different types of worship services, I better understood what I was experiencing. What a blessing it is to know that my love for music and singing is a gift that can bring glory to God. Singing has always been and will always be a source of comfort and fulfillment. In connection with things that brought me fulfillment, the final piece of the triangle, enrolling in a new school, definitely falls in the same category. As

I previously mentioned, my Adoption Summary revealed notes from my Head Start teacher.

She was extremely detailed in her notes about me as a student. That doesn't surprise me because I loved school and I'm sure I was always eager to perform well. Other pieces of documentation disclose that I was in Kindergarten before the adoption, however, because of so many transitions, I did not complete it. When I was enrolled in Norphlet Elementary School, I went directly to the first grade. Attending school has always provided me with a feeling of contentment.

As an adult, I'm able to articulate what I couldn't as a child. School offered so many things that I was longing for: consistency, structure, relationships, stability, and opportunities to experience success. Almost immediately, I was acclimated to my new school, teacher, and friends.

. . . .

School offered so many things that I was longing for: consistency, structure, relationships, stability, and opportunities to experience success.

. . . .

Children who resided in Calion were bussed to Norphlet about 15 miles away. The school was small with a family-like environment. Most (if not all) graduating classes were somewhere around fifty people or less. Primarily, the school was made of students from Calion, Norphlet, and Wildwood (on the outskirts of El Dorado). The student body was made up of a lot of families from those three communities. Several of the teachers and administration were school alumni.

To this day, I don't think I have ever experienced the amount of school pride that was in Leopard Land. I was so delighted to be a part of an awesome educational system. I was apparently so happy about being in school that I made friends easily. In the first few weeks, I was like most children in a new place; a little unsure. But thanks to several chances to go outside for recess and play, I made friends quickly. As a matter of fact, I met my BFF (Best Friend Forever), Jamie! Actually, I could write a book about her and our friendship.

Thirty (plus) years later, we are still best friends! You will hear more about her in the coming pages. When I think back to my first official year of school, I actually only have one bad memory. I guess you could say socializing and building relationships were at the top of my list which was not always done at the appropriate times (recess). One day, I talked a little too much during class, and a teacher made me go into the classroom closet as a punishment. The smell of the absorbent powder that was used for vomit was strikingly overwhelming and even worse than that, it was so dark! I've already mentioned how terrified I was of the dark.

When she shut that door, I started crying uncontrollably. After that didn't get her attention, I had to figure out something so that when I come out of that closet, the whole class wouldn't laugh at me. I looked down and saw a ray of light coming in from under the door. That was all I needed. I laid down flat on my stomach and stared at the light outside of the closet. I counted every shoe, each desk leg, and the floor tiles until she opened the door. When she did, she asked me if I had learned my lesson. Yes, I had! Thankfully, that is my only unpleasant memory of my period of enrolling in a new school. In another chapter, I will share more about my school days.

There you have it, the triangular lifestyle of the majority of my childhood. With everything new: family, church, and school, life was so much different than it had ever been. Those three aspects were never changing. Thankfully, day in and day out, life was predictable. Each night, I slept in the same bed. When I woke up in the morning, I saw the same people. The people didn't change weekly or monthly. Numerous times I've been asked what it was like to be a part of a family that I was not born into.

Separation from my biological family (both maternal and paternal) as a toddler made it difficult for me to answer that question. That was until I grew older and became curious about what was missing and why. During this time, I was glad to say that Monday-Friday, I walked through "the trail" to the bus stop, rode the same bus and attended the same school. Each Sunday, Wednesday, Thursday, and some Saturdays, I attended church services where I was learning how to be a Christian.

Describing these three might give the impression that my journey thus far had finally turned for the absolute better. In several ways, it had. At the same time, in other ways, my new triangular life was far from perfect.

CHAPTER 7

Happily Ever After...?

"For I reckon that the sufferings of this present time are not worthy to be compared with the glory which shall be revealed in us."

— Romans 8:18

I have always been an avid reader. Children's literature will always remain at the top of my list. Specifically, I prefer stories that have a happy ending. I'm sure you're familiar with several fairy tales that end with the phrase, "...and they lived happily ever after."

An educator that I encountered planted this seed. She definitely sparked my interest in reading content with storylines that ended with things working out for the characters. More than likely, my tendency to be optimistic also came from the same place.

Coming from where I've explained and entering a new life that was less than perfect did not always make being positive an easy feat. Put simply, being adopted was not my "happily ever after." When I'm asked about my adoptive parents and living with them, I have to explain my relationship with them in stages - from childhood, adolescence, young adulthood, and then adulthood. In this chapter, I'll primarily share about my childhood; ages 6-12.

There is no doubt that Mama and Daddy provided me with a stable home environment. The primary needs of food, clothing, and shelter were always satisfied. They both worked consistently to make sure of that. As a child, I didn't realize we were somewhere between poor and the lower-middle class. That's how I would categorize us looking back. Like most children, I always looked forward to holidays, birthdays, and special occasions. One of my fondest memories was our first Christmas after adoption.

That Christmas was not only unforgettable because it was the first, but as it was the only one like that.

Christmas came approximately three months after moving to South Arkansas. I had never experienced what we found on that magical morning! When we pulled back the curtain that was in the doorway of our bedroom, not only were presents under the tree, but also covering every couch, chair, and the entire living room floor! The most memorable gift was a doll that stood nearly as tall as me. Her smooth brown skin, straight black hair, and white dress with a pink bow were perfect! When I took her hand, she would "walk" beside me. I loved that doll and everything else I received. That Christmas was not only unforgettable because it was the first, but as it was the only one like that. Each year following that, presents were extremely minimal. One year, I received a single pair of wool socks that were the color of mustard (an ugly yellow). I was so disappointed and confused.

Compared to the initial holiday those that followed were dismal and sad. At some point in my childhood, getting up early to go to the living room was no longer necessary. Honestly, I preferred not to face the disheartening feeling. This explains my current resistance to and struggles with being a seasonal person. Decorating a tree, pulling out holiday-themed décor to turn my home into a winter wonderland and entertaining people are always a strain on my emotions.

After so many years of not celebrating (gifts, toys, etc.), it does not come naturally to me. As an adult, all of this finally made sense to me. I remember Mama telling us that her mother, Big Mama, bought the dolls. She didn't share the other details, but I speculate friends, church members, co-workers, and maybe even the Department of Human Services aided my parents in making sure that we had an amazing Christmas that year. Now,

I can comprehend the true meaning of Christmas and without a doubt celebrate Jesus' birth above all, but as a child, I didn't understand.

The most perplexing thing was that my parents worked; tirelessly. My mother rarely missed work. My dad was always on the road. I now realize they had bills and other responsibilities. I don't believe those obligations kept them from providing us with childhood pleasures. As a matter of fact, it wasn't only at Christmas time that I had this experience. Birthdays, another time that most children look forward to, were rarely celebrated. I remember a couple of my sisters having a birthday party, but I never had one until I was a teenager.

That one party was planned by another one of my sisters and me when we decided to give ourselves a celebration. We ordered pizza and decorated using our own money (earned from babysitting). We excitedly invited friends, but unfortunately, only a couple of them were able to attend. We were upset, but glad to have some type of recognition for our birthdays. Gifts would have been nice but even a simple "Happy Birthday" would have made my day. I'm still convinced that neither of my parents knew my birthday. If I had not mentioned it (every year), it would have easily been overlooked.

There was little to no interest in things that seemed to be so common in other families. These facts made me feel sad during these times of the year. I didn't know what it was called at the time, but I was definitely fighting seasonal depression from an early age. When I would ask why I didn't get birthday presents or Christmas gifts, money (or the lack of) was always the answer. Due to the countless trips to "town," El Dorado, with my mother to handle business on Fridays, I knew there was some money. What I didn't know is that her income was many times the only one being applied to the household because of my dad's habits.

Through the years, he struggled with substance abuse issues on and off. There were a lot of times he came home really late and sometimes not at all. Those nights (or early mornings) always resulted in loud arguing and cursing between my parents. When it would start, two things would happen simultaneously. I would become extremely scared and angry. That was not a good combination!

As a child, I could not explain where the thoughts came from, but immediately I would go into a defensive and protective mode. I believe my early years brought this on. Many nights I slept with a butcher knife under my pillow with the intention of defending my mother if necessary. Mind you, I began this practice as an eight (8) year-old and continued through my early teenage years. My family had no idea the knife was there, and they also didn't know the depth of my anger issues because neither did I. The phrase "see red" does not seem to capture the amount of anger that would take complete control of my emotions.

It would happen so quickly that it would take me and the person (or should I say target) who I was angry with by surprise. On one occasion, I placed the muzzle of a pistol to my older brother's head. He said something that upset me. I returned with the pistol from under my parent's mattress. He was so caught off guard when I walked up behind him and pressed it to his temple. Thank God for His protection! I don't know if that gun was loaded. I didn't have intentions to kill. I simply wanted to make sure my brother knew I was not afraid of him.

Another time, I stormed to a neighbor's house because her grandchildren told me she was going to beat me up. With a butcher knife in hand, I taunted this grown woman (old enough to be my mother) and beckoned for her to come outside. This wasn't smart because when she came to the door, she was pointing a gun at me. Obviously, I realized quickly that I needed to back down. But backing down was not something that came easily for me. When kids would pick on me (girls and boys included), I was always ready to fight.

Although I was always very small, I would use all of my strength and fight until the end. I was determined to make sure no one thought they could harm me without me putting up a good fight. This included family. One fight was with one of my sisters. After a verbal argument, we exchanged a few blows. Actually, she got the best of me (she's among few who can say that), but my anger is what I think about in retrospect. I told her that I would cut her up into little pieces and throw her in the ditch.

Wow! I thank God for deliverance! Most people don't believe me when I talk about how often I fought as a girl and teenager. Actually, I had my last fight as a freshman in college. Again, that fight ended with a double-barrel shotgun being pointed at my head. I had my share of tussles; playing in the yard, walking home from school, while in the bathroom at school, riding on the school bus, and virtually any time someone threatened me.

I wrestled with anger; it was an automatic and uncontrollable emotion that plagued me for so many years. And if it wasn't anger, it was depression. When I wasn't ready to battle, I felt low and defeated. On many days, it was hard to put one foot in front of the other. At times, I think my diagnosis of chronic asthma led to the depression. There were multiple days that I was not able to breathe, gasping for air. High fevers, wheezing, coughing, and what felt like a weight on my chest were common symptoms.

....

I wrestled with anger; it was an automatic and uncontrollable emotion that plagued me for so many years.

....

When I was in foster care, I had asthma, but it wasn't as bad as it was after the adoption. That was largely due to my parent's smoking. That one trigger was something that I could not escape. Both Mama and Daddy smoked in the house, and we had a wood-burning heater to add to that. The asthma attacks would last for days at a time. The depression would creep in during that time. Too many times to count, I would lie in bed while my sisters and the neighborhood kids would be playing right outside the window. I wanted to go out and play too. I felt left out and abandoned. To add to that, several times while I had the attacks, I would be accused of "faking," which made me feel rejected and miserable.

Because I had suffered from this for so long, I always knew when I needed to go to the doctor, but that was always the last resort. Mama would say she didn't have gas money, but I didn't believe her. She and Big Mama would try every remedy (some worked) before making the trip to "town" to see the doctor. I can't tell you how relieved I was to travel those 12 miles to get a breathing treatment! One day after leaving the doctor, I asked Mama why she "told a story," lied to the doctor. When he asked her if she smoked in front of me, she said, "No." Her reply was, "Hush!" and I did.

As a child, I thought she was smoking to make me sick on purpose. The two times my asthma problem was under control came when I was hospitalized. Because I was in a smoke-free environment and treatments were administered correctly, I was able to recover quickly. As far as I can remember, I was the only child in the home that had a condition as severe as asthma. This, among so many other things, made me wonder "Why me?" Without trying, I internalized a lot of things and rarely spoke to anyone about it.

I wrote a lot. My stories were my getaway. Whether I was angry, depressed, or sick, I would escape with my stories that ended in the happily ever after that I longed to have. One of my stories was about a girl who was invisible. She existed, but wasn't visible to her family. Her days were long and grueling as she tried to be a good girl. She did all of her chores. She made everyone laugh by being goofy. Her favorite thing to do was dance and sing. When the family would smile, she was satisfied. But no matter how much she did those things, she always ended up invisible in the moments when she needed to be seen most.

> **Whether I was angry, depressed, or sick, I would escape with my stories that ended in the happily ever after that I longed to have.**

The "invisible girl" was me. I don't know if my family knew it, but I fought with feeling unseen. I recall these emotions being triggered by some things that literally caught me off guard. Quite a few times, my mom would tell me (in secret) that I could go with her to pay bills after work on Friday, but she would not pick me up. After hearing the whistle at the mill, I would watch the clock waiting for her to pull into the driveway.

The minutes on the clock seemed to speed up, and then I'd see the van enter the highway from my bedroom window.

She left me. She promised I could go. This would lead me into a crying fit. For over an hour the cry would intensify to the degree that I had to hide from my sisters so that they wouldn't see me. It was not about going to El Dorado to do the family business. It was the disappointment and rejection that would not stop bothering me.

In those moments, I knew I was a big girl (at least 10 or 11), but I felt like that 4 year old girl again. Going back to the concept of feeling like the invisible girl, maybe I identified with Cinderella. Her unnoticed efforts of cleaning and taking care of everyone led her to feel left out and looked over. In our household, everyone had chores. By the time I was 12, there was nothing that I didn't do. Laundry, dishes, dusting, deep cleaning, sweeping, stacking wood, cooking, lawn work, feeding the dogs, and the list goes on!

I'm a firm believer that chores are needed and necessary to teach life skills, but I believe the level at which I did them surpassed what children should have to do. Over the years, I've decided that this was a child's purpose in the eyes of our parents. For lack of a better description, I felt like a slave.

The list of to-do's was always long and receiving a "thank you" or "good job" was rare. A few of my least favorite memories are taking off my dad's socks, fixing both of their plates and serving them in bed and getting up at very early hours in the morning (3 AM for example) to fix my dad breakfast and lunch before he left for work. Though I knew not to refuse or be slow about doing what was asked, I always felt that my mom should have been the person doing most of these things. There was basically no consideration for the fact that I was a child.

While it's important to teach and train, there is a thin line between appropriate and inappropriate. It was during these times that I resented my parents for adopting me. The list I mentioned above were only the tip of the iceberg. The chores were endless. When I would dare to think about how this was not how it should be, I would be reminded that they kept my sisters and me together. Maybe, just maybe I should be grateful? And with those thoughts, I would check myself and do what I was told.

Besides, if I didn't, there was a price to pay. On that note, I was for the most part "a good kid," very compliant. This was largely due to the discipline that was promised if I wasn't. I'm talking about the kind that is mentioned in the Bible, *"Spare the rod, spoil the child,"* (Proverbs 13:24). Leather belts, switches or small branches from a tree, extension cords, and kindling for the wood-burning stove were used to whoop (not spank) in our household. I received one whooping from my dad - only one!

That was enough. My mom never had to chastise me other than a pop or pinch here or there. She loved to tell the story of how when I was in trouble, I would quickly get down on my knees and start praying loudly. I was begging both the Lord and my mom to extend some grace. It worked too. That's what she gets for introducing me to the Lord.

My only other whooping was more like a beating. It was given to me by my Big Mama. Mercy! I can still remember her cornering me on the porch. I fell on the swing as she stood over me, administering the only childhood correction that still stings to think about. While on the subject of things stinging, when I was nearing the end of childhood, my biological mother contacted my adoptive mother. I don't remember all of the details, but it was a phone call. After being told it was for me, she said, "Hello, Shaneil, this is your mother." I was so confused.

Why did Mama call me to the phone for this?

After over seven years of not hearing from her, my mind had erased her from my memory. Anger overtook me. I replied with, "Who?" She said, "Marsheill, your mother." I replied with, "Oh, hi Marsheill." While she was talking, she continued to so casually call me by my name (Shaneil) - which I did not go by. Shortly after being adopted, I was not called by my name, Shaneil, and I was no longer referred to as "Pinky."

My parents didn't like that name, and since they needed a way to keep all of our names straight, I was given the nickname, "P.J." I will give more explanation about that in the next chapter. If I remember correctly, Marsheill was incarcerated. She tried to make small talk, but I wasn't interested. When I hung up the phone with her, I felt conflicted.

I was angry, depressed, and again was convinced that I must have been unnoticeable. Why would she bring to the surface what my mind had inadvertently forgotten? After her initial call, no one knew it, but I literally wanted to disappear. Unbeknownst to my family, I devised a plan to make that happen. My Big Mama, who I shared a bedroom with, took a little brown pill to help her sleep at night and I figured if it only took one for her, maybe 4 or 5 of them would do the trick. I know what you're thinking, "Do kids even know what suicide is?" The answer is yes. I knew I did not want to live and I thought killing myself was the answer.

Since my happily ever after had not happened and now this ghost from my past was present again, I did not want to face life any longer. That night, I waited until Big Mama was asleep and I poured the smooth brown pills into my hand. Mind you, I hated medicine! I would hide my asthma medicine behind furniture and flush it down the toilet. Each time I hid my medicine, it would be discovered by family members. In that low moment, I didn't see the pills as medicine; I saw them as a way out. I took the pills with a couple of gulps of water and lay in the bed straight as a board. I remember lying there thinking 100 miles per hour.

....

In that low moment, I didn't see the pills as medicine; I saw them as a way out.

....

I kept thinking, "Why am I still alive?" I wondered what everyone would think the next day. I can't remember what month this was, but we were out of school because I woke up late the next morning

(PRAISE GOD!) to a lot of noise outside of the bedroom window.

When I opened my eyes, the room was spinning, and I couldn't stand up. Big Mama noticed as she was sitting on the side of the bed looking at me and she said, "You must not feel good?" I replied with a simple, "No." I stayed in bed and cried most of the day. Later in the afternoon, one of my neighborhood friends came into the house to say hi and asked if I was okay, I gave a lazy wave and said, "Yes." My Big Mama told her my asthma was acting up and I didn't bother to disagree with her.

I wish I could say that overall, my childhood was happy, but looking back it wasn't. No doubt, a lot of positive things occurred. My favorite memories are of my sisters and me pretending to shop from our mom's closet, playing dress up and our all-time favorite, pretending to have church at home. Sharing a room with my Big Mama was fun because she was so entertaining.

Our house seemed to be the hub for the community's kids because our huge yard was perfect for kickball, baseball, and games like "Mother May I?" and "Red Rover, Red Rover!" On the flip side of that coin, my life was like a roller coaster filled with suffering. Not experiencing simple childhood pleasures, having chronic asthma, literally fighting to find my place, being weighed down with inappropriate duties and tasks and feeling like I didn't matter to the people who meant the most to me made life almost unbearable.

At that time, I couldn't imagine life getting any better. Now I can see God's glory revealed through these sufferings, and it is a blessing that I cannot adequately explain. Though I had a pessimistic view of myself and almost everyone in my surroundings, God did give me a way to escape - school.

CHAPTER 8

School Days

*"[God will] make the way of escape,
that [we] may be able to bear it."*

— I Corinthians 10:13

To say "I love school!" is an understatement! I often tell people I love school so much that I went to school at the age of three and never left. For the majority of my life, I've been "in school" in some shape, form or fashion. School has always been my happy place. From childhood through college, without a doubt, it was an "escape" for me. When there, I felt as if I were free! I did not feel confined or under the control of things that seemed to weigh me down.

School has always brought me a sense of comfort. The structured schedule offered predictability. Seeing the same, kind people every day provided security. Numerous opportunities to be successful appealed to my tendency to please. Meeting people and establishing relationships was easy for me. Even the familiar smells of school, the cafeteria food, hallway aroma after recess time, and the easy to identify "school bathroom scent," were weirdly soothing.

My very first school experience was Head Start. I don't recall much except when I would climb up on a small step stool to brush my teeth. The toothbrush had my name on it in big letters: "PINKY." Feeling that sense of ownership was so special. Sometimes I wonder if I had a toothbrush at home (in my biological mom's apartment)? My Head Start teacher would stand behind me, smiling into the mirror, instructing me on how to brush correctly.

Her smile was infectious as she patted me on the back, singing a tune. I wish I could remember her name, but in my opinion, what I can call to mind is more important; the frequency of her warm embrace. A Maya Angelou quote that I adopted and posted in my classroom (and office) many years later still rings true, "People will forget what you said. People will forget what you did. But people will never forget how you made them feel."

I've already mentioned the one bad flashback from school when I was placed in the closet. That instance made me feel scared and unwanted. Thankfully, I did not have that (or anything close to it) ever happen again. Elementary school was where I found my stride! It's baffling to me when people cannot "summon up remembrance of things past" (Shakespeare) as it pertains to school. For me, there are highlights of every grade level.

In first grade, I learned to spell my name correctly and completely. Before my teacher, Mrs. McEachern, pointed out the error, I was spelling it *Shanell*. During the numerous transitions in my early academic years, I had been taught to spell it incorrectly. That's strange, yet not surprising. Many children in foster care are not familiar with the proper spelling of their names. Actually, many are not aware of their full, legal names. That was the case with me.

When she showed me a copy of my birth certificate as proof, I saw my name, *Shaneil Denise Curley*. I was bewildered for two reasons. Firstly, I realized I didn't know my own name. Secondly, how were my adoptive parents, Andrew and Ernestine, on my birth certificate? Truthfully, I'm still investigating the latter, hoping to retrieve a copy of my original birth certificate. I felt so disconnected and perplexed. How could I be nearly seven years old and not know my name?

To add insult to injury, it was (is) frequently mispronounced. Most people think it's like the perfume, Chanel No. 5. In actuality, it is enunciated *Shuh-kneel*. Therefore, to this day, I rarely use my first name. Though it is not as bad as it once was, sometimes, it still seems to carry the sting of a mistaken or unsure identity. Needless to say, my first grade teacher made an impression. Speaking of impressions, it was also in the first grade that I met my "BFF," my Best Friend Forever!

For nearly the last 36 years, one person has been constant in my life, Jamie LaJoyce Benton-Davis. It started on the playground, stretched to our grade school classrooms, and blossomed into a lifetime. I cannot help but echo Oprah Winfrey on friendship, "Everybody needs a Gayle." I am far from being Oprah, but Jamie is my Gayle. Honestly, it's okay if I'm her Gayle. In many ways, she is definitely my Oprah.

I still haven't figured out what I did to deserve her, and I don't know if I ever will. My wish for everyone is that they can have someone like her in their life. In every moment, elementary school through now, without fail, she has been there! We have laughed a lot and cried even more (we're both crybabies), but one thing that makes our friendship special is that we have never had a disagreement!

It may sound like an anomaly, but it's true. God has graced Jamie and me with an innate gift within our bond that has superseded the normal. As we talk about the two of us coming from neighborhoods, Calion and Wildwood, that feuded over the most trivial things, we know our relationship was (is) extraordinary. I like to think of her as my personal doula. A doula is defined as a trained professional who provided continuous physical, emotional, and informational support to a mother before, during, and shortly after birth.

This person, usually a woman, is a supporter and a companion. One of their ultimate roles is to hold the hand of the woman in labor and encourage her to know that there is life after the pain and discomfort. That description could not better explain my BFF. Through it all, she has been non-judgmental and compassionate. Meeting her in first grade was not only monumental but also life-changing.

While in second grade, Mrs. Barnhardt taught me to write in cursive. This led me to write more and more. The curvy motions that created such beautiful letters really enticed the writer in me. To this day, I have more notebooks, journals, and stationery than I can ever use. Some might argue that cursive writing is fleeting; it is still my most favorite type of penmanship. Third grade brought another teacher who was friendly and always encouraging. She was patient with my obvious deficiency in math. The simplest math was so frustrating for me.

Addition, subtraction, and the dreaded multiplication facts were always difficult for me. When it was my turn to stand at the board to "compete with classmates," I think Mrs. Polk would say the facts that I knew. I don't know if she did it purposely or if God was showing me grace, but I felt so much relief. In her class, I was never embarrassed, and she was also very attentive to my health, as I needed to visit the nurse because of complications with asthma.

Learning that skill (saving) became one of the most valuable lessons I've ever learned.

My fourth grade school year was historic. For the first time, my teacher was a black woman, Mrs. Hunter! She was smart, straightforward, well-dressed, and embodied professionalism. I was completely enamored with her. She commanded the attention of the class with her soft, but stern voice and always made me feel like I could conquer anything! One of my favorite memories in her class was saving pennies as a class to spend at the neighborhood store. Learning that skill (saving) became one of the most valuable lessons I've ever learned.

From the next school year, I still have an artifact from Mrs. Dumas' fifth-grade class. It's entitled Interest Inventory. On the worksheet, I wrote in the answers to several questions such as, "What is your favorite color (pink)?" "What is your hobby (singing)?" and "Where would you go on your dream vacation (Hawaii)?" As I've fore-stated, pink is my favorite, singing remains one of my hobbies, and although I haven't been yet, Hawaii is one of my dream vacations.

My most favorite question on the Interest Inventory was, "What do you think you want to be when you grow up (a teacher)?" This now discolored piece of paper serves as an indication that I knew at the age of 9 what I wanted my future to hold. That's indisputable because of the educators I came in contact with in my elementary years. Last, but certainly not least, was sixth grade. This was the year of all things New Kids on the Block (roughly 1988-89)!

All year long, my friends and I were "*Hangin' Tough*" belting out "*Please Don't Go Girl!*" while playing our favorite game, "*Little Sally Walker*," on the playground. What a year! I had another first that year: a male teacher, Mr. Bishop. He was a gentle giant who I always thought looked like

Superman, Christopher Reeve. In fact, he lived up to that title (Superman) when I was hospitalized that year for over a week. He not only brought my homework to the hospital, but also a card from my class and a bouquet of suckers. That was going above and beyond.

I realize it is out of the ordinary for someone to so vividly recall their elementary school days. It comes naturally to me. Did I mention school was my safe place? "Safe Place" is a term I've borrowed from Dr. Becky Bailey's Conscious Discipline. The Safe Place is a center where children can go to change their inner state from upset to composure. For me, attending school every day helped me to not only self-regulate but also to thrive!

This trend continued in high school (in our small school, 7th - 12th grade were in one building). In my five years of high school, there are a plethora of unforgettable moments. Administrators, teachers, coaches, and school personnel like Coach Bolding, Mr. Burson, Mrs. Coston, Miss Jackson, Mrs. James, Ms. Jones, Mrs. V. Lambert, Coach Lucas, Mrs. Sawyer, Miss Talbert, and Mr. Wright were extremely instrumental in me realizing who I was and what I was capable of.

Without going into detail about each of these educators, I'd like to share a comprehensive list of valuable lessons that I learned due to their investments in my life (in no particular order):

- Everyone deserves a chance.

- Your gifts and talents can take you places if you're brave enough to use them.

- Making a bad choice does not mean you are a bad person.

- There is always someone who sees more in you than you see in yourself.

- What seems impossible is achievable with a little hard work and encouragement.

- Never take the easy route.

- Kindness matters.

- If you do what you love, you will never work a day in your life!

I'm unsure if all of the educators who I listed will read this book. Perhaps some of my childhood and adolescent friends will have the opportunity and agree with me about them. Either way, I feel certain that these individuals were God sent into my path. Of all of the places I could have ended up after being removed from my biological family, living in Calion and being transported to Norphlet for school was in God's plan.

While attending school, like most, I had my first childhood crush and a couple of boyfriends. I played basketball for a little while but later found more gratification in being the team manager and photographer. I was involved in several clubs and always did well in class. I had a lot of friends who I still love and get great joy out of visiting with them as adults. Six girls were virtually inseparable: me, Jamie, Danielle, Donna, Tiffany, and Mandy.

In a paper I once wrote, I referred to us as the "Super Six." The topic of the paper was diversity in a group of friends. When I think back to my school days, they all come to mind without hesitation. Even now, over thirty years later, I have fond memories and a special place in my heart for each of them. We, "Super Six," were great friends, but honestly, everyone knew "P.J.!" There are a couple of reasons for that.

To begin with, I was the NHS homecoming entertainment (singing) for six consecutive years. Each year, I auditioned to entertain the queen and her court for the biggest football celebration of the year.

Secondly, I had all kinds of friends: black, white, the popular kids, the nerds, the athletes – everyone! I loved people, and that did not exclude anyone.

One day, I walked into math class to find an expression of my classmate's love for me. The chalkboard was filled with several variations of what "P.J." stood for. The guys in the class had taken quite some time to come up with names like Peanut Butter & Jelly, Pickle Juice,

Performing at Norphlet High School Homecoming ceremonies (age 15).

Pajamas, Plain Jane, and even Puddle Jumper. They all knew what "P.J." really stood for, "Precious Jewel." I had told them that the nickname was a name my adoptive father had shortened because it wasn't something my sisters or friends would ever agree to calling me every day. Nearly forty years later, I strive to live up to my nickname daily and be a "Precious Jewel."

I'll never forget laughing in class that day until I cried. Later that same day, I cried because I felt

Later that same day, I cried because I felt like I mattered to my friends.

like I mattered to my friends. I shared that with one of my favorite teachers, and she said I was certainly a "Precious Jewel" to handle being the brunt of the joke so graciously. Moments like that in school might seem insignificant to others, but they left me with a strong sense of contentment.

As my time in high school came to an end, I knew I had what I needed to make it in the world. From my academic learning to establishing strong relationships with my peers and teachers, I felt prepared for the next step.

Being afforded the opportunity to travel with the different clubs that I was a part of showed me life beyond my normal. On those trips, I experienced eating in restaurants and staying in hotels for the first time.

My BFF and I even had the amazing chance to travel to Disney World and another country, England. I didn't know it then, but now I realize that God was showing me that there was more. And all I needed was a glimpse into the world to know I wanted it.

For several years, I received the perfect attendance award because I rarely missed school unless I was sick. As an honor graduate, I knew I wanted to go to college and study to be a teacher. I felt confident that my school days had provided me with a solid foundation for attaining my dreams and goals. Life at home was sometimes still difficult, but I knew there had to be more!

CHAPTER 9

There Has To Be More

"Now unto him that is able to do exceeding abundantly above all that we ask or think, according to the power that worketh in us."

— *Ephesians 3:20*

Since the inception of my Christian journey, I have been told that God can do anything but fail. Whether in song, scripture, or sermon, the reminder of God's immeasurable ability has always been a consistent theme. After undergoing such a tumultuous life from the time I can remember, this phenomenon of a mighty God was difficult to wrap my brain around. Strangely enough, it was during a lesson (in Jr. High) on reproduction, the journey of a sperm to an egg, which assisted me in realizing the power of God's plan.

The average male produces about 1,000 sperm with every heartbeat. Before the sperm is ready for release, they spend about a week traveling through a winding tube, the epididymis. While in this tube, the sperm goes through a completion process where special effects are added to them which will help them to function better. Keep in mind that a man's body has the capability of storing billions of sperm.

However, if they remain too long, the sperm die. Once discharged, approximately 250 million begin the voyage to the outside of a woman. Even after all of that, studies show that only about 1 in 100 of the sperm makes it to the shelter of the cervix.

To complicate things, the hormonal profile of a woman must be just right to release an egg from her ovaries. The small window of time (a few days) after ovulation is when sperm are allowed inside. Only the strongest and fastest sperm can enter. The cervix is the door to the woman's womb, and then the sperm must take a strategic left or right into the fallopian tubes. Miraculously, only one of a woman's ovaries will discharge an egg in any given month.

Needless to say, it is crucial that the sperm swims into the correct tube. The female body steps in to aid the sperm during this step by contracting muscles and ultimately allowing the sperm inside the fallopian tubes. A mass reduction in sperm has occurred by this point. Only about 6 (out of a billion) have access to the inside. They literally stick to the inside walls of tubes awaiting the one egg to arrive.

Finally, the one egg enters the tube and within a few hours must be fertilized for conception to occur. Research suggests that only a couple of sperm find the strength to swim towards the egg.

Once they approach it, the winning sperm makes contact with the outer exterior of the egg and then the process of forming a new individual begins. Unbelievable!

Those fertility basics are quite complex! Must I remind you that the embryo's expedition has only begun at that point? It is difficult for me to adequately express the impact that the knowledge of this process had on me. As the statement, "You're not here by mistake," was uttered by my teacher, I got it! Surely if God made it possible for my biological mother and father's bodies to go through all of that to create me, there was a reason for my existence!

In my early teenage years, God began to touch my body and heal me of asthma. I fought some of the symptoms while playing basketball in school, but it was nothing like when I was younger. As I felt better, I wanted to be more productive and make some money. At the time, I was not sure of where the urge came from, but it was strong. I wanted more! Much later in life, after meeting my biological father's family, I learned that the Nichols women have a legacy of strong work ethic!

I started babysitting on the weekends. My mom worked with a lot of people in the community and somehow the word got out that I was available. Nearly every Friday and Saturday night, I babysat. For a few hours, I would watch the children in my care. Though neither were a part of my duties, I would also do some light cleaning and prepare small meals. At the end of the night, I was gratified as the parents of the children would share compliments and of course provide payment for my services. It sunk in quickly, when you do well, people notice. I also began saving money. I learned quickly that I had a knack for that!

Outside of one instance, babysitting was one of my most favorite things to do. In that one case, against my better judgment, I allowed the children I was watching to talk me into a four-wheeler ride in the woods. I knew they were acquainted with outdoors, but I did not take into consideration what the weather had been like the days prior.

As we traveled down a wooded path, I noticed mud all around, but I thought that was normal. Moments later, we rode into a ditch and mud began to fly from under the tires. We were stuck! My first four-wheeler ride, with an eight-year-old as the driver, had ended in a disaster. No matter what we tried, we could not get the ATV out of the hole. My heart was pounding. I knew I would be held responsible for this mess and possibly fired.

We were deep into the woods by this time, but the young man seemed to be familiar with his surroundings; I certainly wasn't. He assured me that we did not need to turn around and go back the way we started, but we were close to the main road that would lead us home. It was getting dark, and since I could not imagine walking all the way back through the woods, I trusted him.

I took his hand and his brother's, and we started jogging until I saw a clearing. He was right; the road was really close. We were covered in mud, but I was so relieved! Moments later, we saw headlights. I told the boys to get on the other side of me, onto the shoulder. As the vehicle got closer, I noticed it was slowing down. The gentleman inside asked what we were doing, and I explained that we had gotten stuck and were walking back. He said that he was headed that direction and we could have a ride.

He told the boys to get on the back of the truck and me to get in the cab with him. Once the boys were settled, I climbed in and immediately said, "Thank you so much!" He smiled and said, "You're going to thank me in a minute." I was confused. What did he mean? I thought, he can't mean that. But he did. I could sense it. He had plans to harm me, more than likely, rape me. In that moment, the smell of oil, gas, and alcohol came to my attention.

I knew this would not end well. He was driving slowly, so my first thought was to jump out of the truck. But the boys were with me. I couldn't leave them! I was silent. I was thinking. I scanned the floorboard of the truck for a weapon. Nothing was there. We were close to the house, so initially, I thought it would be okay. When he grabbed my leg and pulled me close to him, it felt like the oxygen left the inside of that truck. He groped the inside of my thigh and began kissing my neck really hard (all while swerving off the road) I was trying to push him off, but he was so strong. My head was spinning, and my heart felt as if it would jump out of my chest.

After a struggle, I managed to get away from him. I scooted over to the other side of the truck and began clinging on to the door handle. He asked me if I was going to jump out and I said, "Yes!" He laughed and said I was a "stupid little black girl" (he was an older white man) and that I would die. I replied by telling him that I would rather die than be in that truck with him. Then he slammed on the brakes and said, "Get out!" And that is what I did! I helped the boys off of the back of the truck and told them we would walk the rest of the way. They were asking questions, but I was not responding. I only wanted to get them home and for all of us to be safe.

When we entered their house, I instructed them to take a bath and go to bed. The rest of the night, into the early morning hours when their parents arrived, I cried. That evening had been more than I could have ever imagined. Once they were home, I explained about the four-wheeler incident and apologized profusely. I also told them that I could not accept payment for the evening because I knew I had made a bad decision. They appreciated my honesty and insisted on paying me anyway. However, that was my last time. The trauma of the evening, especially the threat of rape that I never told anyone about, was too much for me. As much as I loved babysitting and those boys, I walked away hoping to find another means of making money.

Within a few months, I found work again, working at a local restaurant, the Kozy Kitchen. I was fourteen years old (too young to be employed) and was paid $40-$60 cash for each night of work (Thursday -Saturday). My duties included: dishwashing, preparing salads, bussing tables, and waiting tables. This job brought both an increase in duties and compensation. It also proved something that I had discovered while attending school. I loved people! I thoroughly enjoyed working with all of the staff (one of my sisters worked there too), and I loved the customers too. I worked hard and took great pleasure in becoming familiar with the regulars. I was tiny in stature, smiled a lot, and was eager to serve. The tips I received were generous, and I loved putting my money away and watching it grow. I worked that job during the summer months, and I had a goal. I wanted to save enough to buy my own school clothes and a really nice backpack. Of course, school was an incentive because it was my happy place!

At the end of summer months, I had accumulated an impressive little stash. I shared my aspiration of purchasing my own school clothes and supplies with my mom, and she said that was a good idea. When we arrived at K-Mart, I was so excited! One of the first items I found was a plaid overall dress. I quickly put it in my shopping cart. I continued gathering everything on my shopping list and was ready to check out. I felt so independent and accomplished!

Before we made it to the cash register, my mom asked me how much money I had, and I told her. I thought she was asking to make sure I had enough to cover my bill and I assured her that I did. That was not her reason for asking. She followed up that question with an instruction that I was not prepared for. My mom told me that I needed to buy one of my sisters some clothes too. I asked, "Why?" Her response was, "If you want that stuff, you will buy her some clothes too, or I will take that money." My heart sank! I didn't understand.

All through the summer, I had been big-hearted. If I ordered a cheeseburger from Mr. Joe B's/Clara's Sandwich Shop, I bought something for everyone. When we went to the Cracker Box (the neighborhood service station) or Mrs. Sue's Grocery (the local grocery store), I always shared with whoever was around, especially my sisters. I was always charitable by nature. That's why I could not comprehend why I was being commanded to make these purchases. But I did. I wanted my items badly enough that I made the sacrifice.

I forfeited having much left over and in my opinion took on a major responsibility which was my parent's, not mine. I lamented over my mom's action for many days and weeks. As much as I loved my job, I despised the day that I had ever gone to work only to have my earnings taken from me. At the time, I thought it was cruel and unusual punishment. I still don't agree with what happened, but I did have a change of mindset because of it. I continued working over the next several years, but I knew if I was going to reap the benefits of my labor, I had to devise a plan to get away. I did not do all of that hard work just to be defeated in the end. I longed to progress!

I did not do all of that hard work to be defeated in the end. I longed to progress!

These happenings pushed me to seek a way to be employed within a career I loved. I wanted to work, save, and enjoy life. Being that I was an older teen now, graduation was near. My junior year of high school was challenging as I was striving to get good grades and stay focused. The coursework was not too difficult, but competing with the magnitude of intelligence in my class was. There were at least five individuals deadlocked for the valedictorian spot, several others in line for salutatorian and a long line of people for the overall top rankings in the group. I knew if I did not get a scholarship, I would be stuck!

To add to challenges in my junior year, one of

my sisters, who was on target to graduate high school that year, was pregnant. Bearing in mind the number of teenage pregnancies that result in high school drop-outs, her sticking in there was to be commended. Unfortunately, that was not the way that people chose to look at the situation. Truthfully, she was not the only girl in her class pregnant. If I remember correctly, there were at least three others and several more within the high school population.

Looking back, it seemed to be an epidemic. Teenage pregnancy was at an all-time high across the nation. This was a wake-up call to me for a couple of reasons. Firstly, I found myself standing up for my sisters and her friends. The talk or should I say gossip about them infuriated me! Their choices were not popular, but they were also not anyone's business. I made sure everyone who was bold enough to say something in my presence knew that.

I desired to be a teacher and the only way to do that was to attend college.

At the same time, I was watching and learning. Witnessing my sister go through a pregnancy and enter motherhood as a teen was the extra push I needed to make some crucial decisions.

While she was an amazing mother and graduated on time, I observed the struggle firsthand. I wanted to do things differently. I desired to be a teacher and the only way to do that was to attend college.

My senior year of high school is one of the highlights of my academic career. I had completed the majority of the required credits, so most of my day was spent in electives with journalism being my favorite. In this class, I was able to do two of my favorite things: write and take photographs. The Norphlet High School 1996 yearbook will always be one of my prized possessions because of the number of articles and photos that I contributed. With an easy academic load that year, I started exploring options for after graduation.

Sadly, there was no support or encouragement from home to pursue college. Every time I brought it up, the same response was given; there was no money for me to attend college. After numerous visits to the high school guidance counselor, I left with little information and always seemed to "miss out" on applications and deadlines. I don't have concrete evidence, but I believe I had already been pre-judged based on two things: my inability to measure up to the scholars within my class and the decisions of others who had come before me. My two older sisters and I graduated 3 years in a row. Whether they were trying or not, school personnel definitely compared me to them. Additionally, in my opinion, some of the people on staff at school showed favoritism to selective students.

My mom talked me into making my senior year purchases (from money I saved) to avoid accruing the cost. She said if I wanted special things, I would have to buy them. When I complained that I wouldn't have any money left over, she offered to pay a $50 deposit and said that was all she would do. While I appreciated that, I quickly became aware of the value of a dollar because the items were quite expensive.

I didn't buy much, but even so, I found great self-satisfaction in purchasing my class ring, senior memorabilia, and senior pictures. In spite of the memories of not having proper parental support during such a significant time, I still hold each of those items dear to my heart. The days seemed to creep by because the only thing I could think of was graduating and going to college.

Finally, my much anticipated high school graduation day came! I was so excited to put on my graduation gown and remember distinctly making sure that I practiced my smile in the mirror. After the graduation ceremony, I was faced with the same question several times, "What are you doing after graduation?" My confident reply was always the same, "I'm going to college. I want to be a teacher!"

Attending college was definitely my intention, but I knew I would have to work really hard to make that a reality. Besides, my parents had made it clear they could not send me to college. Securing transportation to the Kozy Kitchen became a little more difficult for me, so I started exploring other options. The obvious choice was Calion Lumber Company (CLC), the hub of the mill-town. Nearly half of the population was employed there. Both of my parents and my older, adoptive brothers had been employed there.

At the time, my mom was still a saw operator. When I told her I wanted to apply there to save money, she was so excited! She was very happy because "finally" one of her girls would be working at the sawmill. In her eyes, this was the best option. I like to refer to this as "mill-town mentality." With CLC at the center of the community, almost every resident had someone employed there. Needless to say, it was (and still is) a huge source of income. For that reason, my mom thought this was where I should be, instead of college. Of course, I had other plans, but I did not argue with her because I needed her as a reference. After all, she had been there for over twenty years!

The application process and short interview provided for a seamless entry into my third job: stacking wood as it came out of a large saw. The two women operating the saw had been there for years and had watched me grow up. Everyone employed there knew me as one of the "Curley girls." Most people who know me know that I have always been a morning person. Every day since I can remember, I have literally put my feet on the floor (almost immediately) after opening my eyes. Most days, my bed is neatly made within minutes, and I'm off!

Getting up for work at the mill was no different. The excitement of something new, and more importantly, the anticipation of a paycheck made the early mornings really easy. I loved packing my lunch and mama's. While the sun was still rising, we would get in the van with a few others who rode with us for the short drive (less than 5 minutes away). We clocked in while the mill was still relatively quiet and just moments later, it was busy, loud, and above all else, hot! By 9 a.m. (two hours in), the heat was almost unbearable.

I wore shorts and a tank top almost every day, but that didn't make a difference. From where I stood to stack the small furniture pieces exiting the machine, I could see people all around, pouring with sweat. Towels were draped around their necks, water coolers in hand and large industrial fans were all around, but there was no relief. It didn't take me long to realize this was not the type of work environment I wanted!

That fact became my fuel to go to work for the next couple of months as the temperatures rose steadily. I had a goal in mind. I needed enough money to supplement financial aid. That was my motivation. During my lunch breaks, I would call Henderson State University (HSU), speaking with them about what I needed to do to complete my application process. HSU was one of the only colleges I had visited while on a high school field trip.

I fell in love instantly! After learning that a few of my high school teachers were alumni, I knew it was the place for me. With every call, I made a list of things that I needed to do. Following those conversations, I meticulously sought out ways to make it all happen. Unfortunately, discussions with my parents about attending college always ended with me feeling downhearted. Their position was clear: I should forget about college and work at Calion Lumber Company. That was not what I wanted to hear. Without being disrespectful, I continued to explain that I would find a way to go to college!

One summer afternoon at the mill, I bent over to add a few pieces of the wood to my pallet. When I stood up, the metal building was spinning, and I was gasping for air. I was having an asthma attack for the first time in a long time, and my airway was closing quickly. The last thing I remember is walking towards the restroom. A few minutes later, I was found on the floor.

I had passed out from the heat and lack of air. I was rushed to the hospital and treated for both asthma and heat exhaustion. The doctor ordered a few days off. At the end of day three, my mom came home and told me I had been released.

The foreman informed her that my illness was a risk they weren't willing to take. My last check was brought to me and added to what I had accumulated while employed there. Honestly, I can't say that I was sad to leave the mill, but I was worried about my chances of leaving in about a month and a half for college. How would I afford to go to college? Like always, God had a plan that I had not imagined.

After sharing what had happened with my Pastor and his wife (Pastor and 1st Lady Williams), they asked if I'd be interested in helping with their children (and small chores) while they worked. The arrangement would require me to move to Camden and live upstairs in their home (the set up was similar to a small apartment). They offered to pay me for my services, which would help with my savings for college. Perfect! I already had experience with babysitting (I had missed working with children), I knew how to cook, and I loved to clean.

I moved in with them and traveled home to Calion for church on the weekends. I enjoyed this time immensely! My pastor's wife was a teacher, and she was always eager to share with me about the profession. My pastor worked for the school district, so he had valuable insight too. They were in full support of my dream to attend college and volunteered to help me in any way they could. That was exciting and refreshing! To add to the excitement, I received my acceptance letter to Henderson! I was on cloud nine. I could feel my dreams getting closer!

My only roadblock was getting my financial aid paperwork submitted. In addition to numerous calls, I received countless documents in the mail.

Bear in mind, this was prior to everything being easily accessible online. All of the paperwork had to be filled out by hand and mailed. Deadlines were in place and could not be missed. Even with knowledge of that, my parents refused to give me a copy of their tax documents. Information about their income was a huge part of the required documentation. Without it, my application was incomplete. In the end, this resulted in me not being able to attend Henderson. I was crushed! My heart was broken! Moreover, I thought I was stuck, again. I had no idea that my pastor had family members and friends who worked at the community college, Southern Arkansas University Tech (SAU Tech).

Our many conversations about my aspirations led them to talk to their connections. First, I was given an application for SAU Tech and then information about a minority scholarship that was specifically for an education major. Next, I was told extensive instructions on how to become an 'independent student.' Then, I completed all of the paperwork with one-on-one assistance. Did I mention I did not ask for any of these things?

During that short time, I was introduced to the favor of God. My personal definition of favor is unsolicited kindness or approval. How do you know if you have obtained this favor? Consider this: you don't look for it, you can't imagine it, but it finds you. As I began my journey to a college that I had never heard of, on a scholarship I didn't ask for, I grasped that I was a beneficiary of God's favor! He certainly had gone beyond what I expected.

....

My personal definition of favor is unsolicited kindness or approval.

....

It still blows my mind how that kind, loving group of people (some who didn't know me) came together to help me. I worked to retrieve the letters of recommendation, wrote essays, and shared my unusual circumstances with a committee in order to change my status. Just in case that sounds easy, it wasn't. The embarrassment of explaining my parent's refusal to help me attend college was hard enough to face without restating it multiple times. The awkward looks of disbelief made me cringe. I was so relieved to receive a letter of acceptance from SAU Tech.

Soon after, my financial aid was awarded with enough to provide on-campus housing. The scholarship award letter, which covered all other expenses, was icing on the cake! While this was unfolding, I was in disbelief, but so grateful. With August approaching, I began packing and collecting items that I needed. Since my parents were not on board with me attending college, all my help came from outside sources.

My pastor's family, church family, and friends rallied together to prepare me for college. Late that summer, I began visiting a church where a guy I was dating attended. Even though they didn't know me well, they also assisted. His mom, in particular, was very encouraging. She told me she wanted me to reach my goals because she had never had that chance. Her attitude demonstrated what I longed for from my own parents.

Disappointingly, that didn't happen. It didn't occur to me then, but now I fully understand that neither of them had a college education. On top of that, my two sisters who graduated before me had chosen different paths. They were both married and had entered the busy life of working and motherhood. I was different. I wanted something out of the ordinary. That reality was not easy for my parents to accept.

Nonetheless, without a doubt, I knew there was more to life than what they wanted for me. Thankfully, God strategically provided me with every resource that I needed to attend college! He placed the right people in my path. He deliberately caused some things to fall through. When I thought it was over, He gave me a fresh opportunity. Provision came from unexpected places and sponsorship from the most unlikely sources.

Today, whatever you are facing, be encouraged. It's not over. There is more to come! Your current situation is not a permanent position! God has a plan. He's in control. Trust Him to send the right people, establish the provision, and thrust you into your predestined future!

CHAPTER 10

The College Years
- Part I

*"Do not be conformed to this world, but be
transformed by the renewal of your mind, that by
testing you may discern what is the will of God,
what is good and acceptable and perfect."*

— Romans 12:2

Since grade school, Friday (or at least by the middle of the week) was a test day. Spelling tests were my favorite and math tests were my nemesis. Regardless of whether I was prepared or not, the tests were inevitable. Maybe you've heard the phrase, "When God starts blessing, the devil starts messing." Realizing my dream of attending college was proof of this popular phrase. Although it was the right choice, it seemed to be the trigger for many things going wrong for me.

Looking back, I learned that life's toughest circumstances are given by God to assess (test) a person's integrity and submission to God's will and His word. On college move-in day, I rode with my pastor's family to East Camden, Arkansas. I was so thrilled! Little did I know, things were about to change. The support

Looking back, I learned that life's toughest circumstances are given by God to assess (test) a person's integrity and submission to God's will and His word.

I had from them was about to end due to horrible rumors that had begun to spread. "They" (church people) said my Pastor was being kind to me with inappropriate intentions. It had even been said that he and I were in a relationship.

Of course, none of the allegations were true! Woefully, all of the help that they had extended ended in heartbreak because of the slander that was being spread throughout the church. He decided to address it one day (over the microphone in a church service), which brought me a great amount of shame. That weekend was their final time transporting me from Calion to Camden. I'll never forget that trip because it was strangely silent. When we made it to SAU Tech, they helped me unload my items.

As we retrieved the last items from their vehicle, his wife, children, and I quietly said our goodbyes. My pastor helped me take the final items to my apartment. He wished me well and told me to let them know if I needed anything. After closing the door behind him, moments later, there was a knock on the door. I figured I had left something by accident. When I opened the door, my pastor was standing there with an odd expression on his face. He seductively looked at me and said, "All those things they said about us... did you want them to be true?" I can only imagine what my face looked like because I was horrified! With tears in my eyes, I said "No!"

I closed the door hurriedly and immediately slid down on the floor right behind the door. Oddly enough, in the pit of my stomach, I felt the same disgust that I had felt in the truck years before with the strange man. Much like he was supposed to be helping me, my Pastor's assistance now seemed to have an invisible string attached to it. I had done nothing wrong, but I felt responsible. I wondered if I had done anything to solicit his flirting.

Deep down, I was certain I had not, but I was so confused at the time; I felt violated. And I wondered if anyone (men specifically) could be trusted to be there for me genuinely without inappropriate expectations being attached. At that point, I lost faith in my spiritual leader and decided I wouldn't get close to another one again. My first pastor (whom I adored) had passed away, and this one had broken my trust.

That was the end of my contact with their family until many years later. Separation was necessary because I was not strong enough to face them. His wife, in particular, had been so kind, and I did not want to feel the awkwardness when in her presence. Consequently, I inadvertently added them to the list of people who entered and exited my life. There I was, in a place I had always dreamed of being, and all I could do was cry. I wept for hours as I felt a combination of emotions overflow; betrayal by those who I trusted, happiness because I was finally in college, sadness due to the rejection I felt from my parents, and fear for the uncertainty of whether I would be able to succeed.

Thankfully, I was dropped off with the basic essentials to be settled for, roughly the first month of class. The apartment had two bedrooms that locked from within, as well as a kitchen and bathroom that were shared with a roommate. When I arrived, my roommate was not there; however, her bed was made, and she had several items in the common areas. When I saw all of the groceries in the kitchen, I initially thought they came along with the apartment, but later learned that her family had made sure she had plenty to last for a while. Next door was another young lady who also had contributed to the food and snack supply. I immediately felt guilty for not bringing much food. I was already prepared to eat lightly until I was able to get more.

To my surprise (and relief), both of my roommates were open to sharing anything they had. When meals were cooked, everyone was welcome to eat. I was happy to help with food preparation and often volunteered to do the cleanup. A few weeks into classes, my roommate (assigned to the room with me) began to disappear frequently. At first, it was for a day or two, but then for extended amounts of time. I later found out she decided college was not for her.

She came one day while I was in class to gather her things and left me a note stating that I could have everything she had left behind. The items included bedding, toiletries, food, and some clothing. I felt like Ruth, the widow in the Bible, who was harvesting in the field of Boaz. In Ruth, Chapter 2, she is depicted as a "gleaner." After Boaz saw her, he showed her favor, and she never wanted again. Like Boaz had instructed his field workers to leave extra behind, it was as if these things in the apartment had been left behind on purpose!

As a matter of fact, I know they were. While I waited for my financial aid refund, things became tough and tight! I gleaned all of my former roommate's abandoned items. This provided me with basic necessities like food, soap, tissue, deodorant, detergent, etc. Thanks to those items and a kind young lady in the adjoining room, I was able to make it through the first full semester of college.

While attending SAU Tech, I was somewhat secluded. The college was located in an industrial area with very little traffic after school hours. I did not have transportation, so I rarely left the college. My parents made it clear that they weren't willing to make the 40-mile trip. When I did leave campus for the weekend, it was to visit my boyfriend's family. After finding a ride to El Dorado, his mom and family served as a refuge during that time.

I was only 12 miles from my parent's home, but was spending less and less time there. As a matter of fact, after leaving for college and not being able to come home for several weekends, my mom told me to, "Stay where you are since you're too good to come home." For some reason, she couldn't understand that I wasn't avoiding coming home; I didn't have a way to get there.

One thing I missed about home was attending church on the weekends. A few churches in Camden would send their church buses to pick up students, but it wasn't every Sunday. When visiting my boyfriend's mom, church attendance was a given! I went with her to several services when I was in town, sometimes three times in a weekend. Their church, Wesson St. Church of God in Christ, was what I had known as "sanctified." My only experience with this kind of church had been underneath a tent in our community when I was a young child.

This church was not what I was used to, but I liked it! The way they worshiped reminded me of what I felt when I started singing in the choir as a young girl. That familiar feeling that seemed to bubble up with no warning was back! The only difference is that it was almost during the entire church service. The energy-level of worship was high! This style of charismatic worship was completely new to me.

The church was "a hand clapping, foot stomping, tongue talking" church! When I attended church there, my emotional battles seemed easier to handle. The tears I shed while there were not the same. Both the preacher and the people in the congregation were always encouraging me to "give it to God." My pain (from that present time and my past) would come to mind, but being in God's presence would take the edge off!

Although I enjoyed attending this new church, I will admit there were several things I was working on and through. After beginning college and not being able to go home for the weekends, I began finding things to occupy my time. Some things I was invited to do, others I decided to experiment with, and in a few instances, I gave into peer pressure. Invitations to out of town trips (as far as four hours away) to explore loud and crazy dance clubs came often. I loved to dance, so I rarely turned down the opportunity! When I think back to all of those trips up and down the road, I can't help but thank God for His protection. Imagine this: older teens and young adults packed in vehicles with more people than there were seat belts, traveling at high speeds (late nights and early mornings) with drivers who had been drinking alcohol. That was not smart! We obviously didn't think through what the outcomes could have been.

. . . .

When I think back to all of those trips up and down the road, I can't help but thank God for His protection.

. . . .

Besides loving to dance, I also liked drinking. This is one example of my experimenting stage. Honestly, at the time, I had no idea why drinking came so natural to me. Hard liquor, sweet liquor, mixed drinks - I liked it all. When people asked if

I could really handle a particular drink, I would definitely prove I could. There were times when I drank so much it wasn't fun anymore. In spite of my small frame and low body weight, I could "hold my liquor."

I danced longer and laughed louder, but I only drank myself sick a few times. After hugging a toilet for half a day, a couple of times, I learned my lesson. I did not know at the time that my high tolerance for alcohol consumption was hereditary. I couldn't explain it then, but now I can; both of my biological parents struggled with alcoholism. The expression, "The apple doesn't fall far from the tree," can actually sometimes be true. Praise God for reaching down and picking the apple (me) up and dusting me off!

Finally, peer pressure was a distraction. Somehow I avoided any major peer pressure while in high school. Having good friends from great families made a big difference! The majority of us were brought up in Christian homes, and we held each other accountable. To add to that, my awkwardness, small stature, and strict parents made it almost impossible to get into much. There was one guy I had a crush on for years (he was about two years older), but we never really dated.

Telephone calls were the extent of our courtship. My one real boyfriend in high school was allowed to visit our home. We were eventually given the chance to go out a little, but mostly, he spent a lot of time with my family. It may be viewed as "old school," but parents and siblings being present helped to keep us on track. Note: that still works today! Now, don't get me wrong, I tried a few things, but it didn't get interesting until I was attending college. The absence of supervision and restrictions ultimately led to temptations that I failed to resist.

Venturing out to this new place of freedom introduced me to new people and new relationships.

Venturing out to this new place of freedom introduced me to new people and new relationships.

The young man that I seriously began to date was only a little older; however, much more experienced. His mother was the lady who I went to church with often. She had reared him and his siblings alone, and in my opinion, had done an excellent job. He was kind, funny, and always very complimentary. He knew my struggles from home and was always there to listen. The one thing that made him different from the other two guys I had liked was his flattery.

I had never been told I was "pretty." Frankly, I had not even thought about it. While some of my friends tell stories of how their parents would often tell them that they were beautiful, my parents did not. My mother would always encourage me to be neat and clean, but she never built my self-confidence. I know for a fact my dad never said anything about my appearance. Therefore, when I heard it for the first time, it was both comforting and appealing. Looking back, some of his compliments were likely being powered by the characteristics of teenage boy charm, but they worked. It made me feel better and gave me a sense of being accepted. I had longed for attention for a long time. The deficiency of attentiveness had left a deep void. Before I knew it, I was engaged in sexual activity attempting to fill that emptiness.

I was so naive. My inexperience united with my low self-worth caused me to fall into a trap. This happens to many young girls. They fall prey to the devil's deception. He is so cunning. He meticulously sets things up to cause girls to believe they are only loved if a young man wants their body. When they have not been properly built up by those who should love and encourage them, they are easily enticed. Without knowing it, they begin to tear themselves down with erratic, unsafe behaviors. Had I known then that I was fearfully and wonderfully made (Psalm 139:1), I would have done things much differently.

Mothers, fathers, teachers, mentors, counselors, caregivers, please do not neglect any opportunity to tell your child (especially girls) that they were fashioned in perfection. Regardless of their reflection in the mirror, when God created them, He saw they were good (Genesis 1:31).

His plan is for them to love themselves as He loves them. In this sex-filled society that we live in, there is an urgency to have conversations, the tough ones!

My parents never talked to me about sex. Occasionally, Mama would make an allusive remark or hint about staying away from boys and "keeping your legs closed," but that was the extent of the dialogue. Those innuendos were not enough! Entering the dating world without proper knowledge was like getting ready to erect a structure with no tools in my tool belt. I was unequipped. Due to my ignorance, I was reeled into deep waters. Before I knew it, I was no longer in the shallow end, but dangerously entering territory I was not prepared to handle.

It was actually a good thing that I didn't get a chance to travel back and forth to visit my boyfriend or my partying crew too often. This way, I was able to focus on what was important, my school work. There was no doubt I knew why I was there and what it would take for me to be academically sound. Although I was enjoying college-life, during class hours, I kept the center of my attention on doing what was necessary.

I knew my scholarship had been awarded as a blessing and I did not want to do anything to compromise that. I thrived in all of my classes. The coursework was interesting, and the faculty and staff were encouraging. Technical (junior) college was exactly the right speed for me. It reminded me of my high school. The atmosphere had a family-like feel. Walking in and out of the buildings, I saw the same faces each day and connected easily to my peers.

I had the same classmates in several of my classes and became close-knit with a few of them. We helped each other with assignments, had great discussions, and found commonalities in ourselves even though we were from different backgrounds. One of my instructors, Mrs. Sutton, had a lot to do with that. It did not take long for her to be added to the list of great educators who made a huge impact in my life. Her passion for teaching was magnetic, and her smile was reassuring. She would challenge us, but at the same time boost our confidence. I had always enjoyed reading and writing, but that quickly blossomed into a deep love for English Literature and English Composition! Though two very common prerequisites, I looked forward to attending class. So much so that I fell in love with Mrs. Sutton too!

I don't remember exactly how it happened or what transpired to set it in motion, but she and I developed a great relationship. She became my "College Mom" and I her "College Daughter." A few of my classmates and I would spend a lot of time in her office and even joined her for an occasional "lupper" as she called it, lunch and supper combined. This was one of the first times I realized how I seemed to gravitate to women who were willing to "mother" me.

My connection with Mrs. Sutton reminded me of my childhood pastor's wife, two teachers from high school, my boyfriend's mom, and even my best friend's mom. They all had this in common; they loved me and cared for me like I was their own. I am so grateful that God deliberately placed all of them in my life at the right times! I don't know if they knew what I was lacking, but it seemed as if they did.

At the time, I rarely talked about being abandoned by my biological parents. I was also too embarrassed to share about my estranged relationship with my adoptive parents. Without a doubt, God knew. Evidently, a mother's intuition can be utilized with children she did not bare. All of these ladies proved that. Whether I was feeling up to it or not, I went to class to see my "College Mom." As time went on, I was able to tell her my truth without being judged. She was truly there for me in some of my darkest days, and 22 years later, we are still in touch!

During my Tech days, many times I had little or no food. When the food was low in the kitchen, and my roommate went home on the weekends, I was hungry. If bread and butter were in the kitchen, I ate toast for all three meals. If not, I ate dry cereal or saltine crackers. My last resort was drinking as much water as I could to fill my belly. I know it's healthy for you, but I've never been a fan of water. There was not a cafeteria on campus, and I had no money.

If I had money, I didn't have transportation to go to the one gas station located about a mile away. I was too ashamed to ask the neighboring residents. They were students, and I'm sure they had their own struggles. I did not share this with teachers because they were already helpful in other ways. Phoning home was not an option because it had been made clear that nothing was coming from there. A few times, I told my best friend (who was back at home working) that I needed help. Without fail, Jamie would either send me money or make sure I had exactly what I needed.

One of my older sisters also sent me care packages. When I visited my college friend's families, they always made sure I was included in whatever they did for them. It may not be something that everyone has to face, but I am a witness that college students can have a rough time. Besides the academic responsibility, fending for basic necessities can be quite stressful. More than once, I fell into a deep depression and did not attend classes for several days all because I was without the essentials. That was both a distraction and a disappointment.

Thankfully, after some time, an instructor on campus decided to take on the task of re-opening the cafeteria. This meant two things for me: food and employment! From day one, I had been signing over my Pell Grant funds to cover the cost of college. Working in the "SAU Tech Sizzler" was a godsend! The paychecks were minimal, but always enough to buy personal items, Ramen noodles, Town House crackers, Vienna Sausages, and Kool-Aid to have in my apartment for the weekend. I know that doesn't equate to a five-star meal, but when you're hungry, it tastes just as good! The cafeteria project was only temporary, but it was a welcomed rain after a dry season. But each time I came across a miracle, a mess would follow.

When we were told the food service personnel would no longer have their positions, I knew I had to save what I could for hard times. After getting a few things with my last check (which was much less), I took a $5 bill and tucked it into my pillowcase. I knew I could not buy much for that amount of money, but I knew I would need it later. That $5 remained there for over a month. The summer months were approaching, and we were informed that the apartments would be closing. Living in the SAU Tech apartments was so much fun! We were a little family.

There were many nights when everyone had their apartment doors open, facing the infamous picnic tables in the middle. Several nights we stayed up all night talking and laughing. Almost every evening was filled with everyone talking noise to each other while playing spades. Most of my free time was spent either talking with the girls (who had become like college sisters) or sitting around the domino table with the guys. They always played for a little money. Before I knew it, I was gambling. Although I didn't have money to contribute, after a few of them learned that I was stiff competition, they made me their partner.

Receiving half of the winnings added up! Thinking back, we were doing what was necessary to keep ourselves entertained. Leading up to our last few weeks there, we all knew we would be going our separate ways, but I'm glad to say in that group of people, I found at least three long-time friends: Angela, Latosha, and Michelle. God had again strategically allowed me to cross paths with people who would later be instrumental in my life. Besides having to part ways with them, the apartments closing meant I wouldn't have anywhere to live while finishing up my last semester.

What would I do? Where would I go? How would I continue my classes? Was this going to be the end for me? I definitely thought so. A friend who was moving a few miles down the road, to an off-campus apartment complex, would further prove that God truly supplies all needs. I met Angela at SAU Tech, and we quickly became friends. She was always friendly, reserved, and seemed mysteriously cautious of people. Being that my personality is the absolute opposite, being as close as we were was not likely. I honestly cannot remember if I asked or if she offered, but I am sure I told Angela I had nowhere to live.

Nearing the end of my two years at SAU Tech, she allowed me to live with her and one other roommate. Since they were the contributing parties, they each took a bedroom while I gladly slept on the comfy, tan colored sectional couch. I did not have a job or any other type of income, but I was eager to utilize the skills that had been drilled into me as a child. I earned my stay by cooking, cleaning, and doing whatever I could to be helpful. Angela also allowed me to drive her to work and use her car to get to class and do school-related tasks. During that time, she and her family treated me like family, and we are still in touch today.

I'm of the opinion that Angela (drop the "a" at the end) was sent as an Angel to lend a hand while I was completing my Associate's Degree. Her acts of kindness ultimately made it possible for me to get to the finish line. When I received confirmation that I had completed all of the requirements for graduation, I was overjoyed! I called my parents, my boyfriend, and Jamie. As expected, Jamie told me she would be there. My boyfriend expressed he wasn't sure if he would attend, but that was okay with me because we were already on the rocks and seeing very little of each other. My mom said that she and dad had to work so she would not make any promises. I asked them to come if they could and hung up the phone, unsure of whether they would be there or not.

Being that my make-up naturally strives for accomplishment, I was on a high the day I was set to receive my degree. I wore a white cap and gown in my high school graduation and a beautiful, royal blue, for SAU Tech. While sitting there with my classmates, I did not look back at the crowd because I wanted to enjoy the moment. Regardless of who was there, or not, I knew the struggle was finally paying off. I was halfway to my dream of being a teacher. The process of transferring to the university from this junior college was uncertain, but somehow I knew it would happen.

God had proven Himself to me over and over

again. To my surprise, during the ceremony, I was awarded a scholarship for future educators that would allow me to transfer seamlessly to Southern Arkansas University, Magnolia. The shocking part is that I did not apply for this honor. It was presented to me via the recommendations of several of the faculty and staff members. I was both surprised and honored!

At the end of the ceremony, the sea of people slowly parted as Jamie and her daughter, my goddaughter, Alandria, made their way to me. Jamie has always been close during my special moments. Her tight hugs that pull me in close around the neck are always reassuring. She doesn't have to say anything because the

Southern Arkansas University Tech graduation (1998).

tears in both of our eyes say it all. Those tears are ones of joy. The joy that she and I always spoke of in high school: *Weeping may endure for a night but joy comes in the morning* (Psalm 30:5)!

I briefly thanked my boyfriend's family for coming. Although we were awkwardly on bad terms, their support was appreciated. Then, I saw my mom standing off to the side. I was instantaneously relieved. They came! As I got closer, I saw my mom and two other family members (not my dad). With a huge smile on my face, I jokingly flashed the degree cover and scholarship certificate at them. As I reached out to hug her, she made two abrupt statements, "Your daddy had to work. I missed work to come see you get this piece of paper, we're leaving."

Immediately, tears fell again, but these were not of joy. I stood there mute; I had no words. As I watched the back of her white dress walk away, I was perplexed. I thought this would be enough to make her proud. Something in me longed to please her and to make her proud of me, but that seemed impossible. After several moments of being consoled by my friends, I skipped the reception that was being held for graduates.

That significant day ended like many others had, with me feeling insignificant. Rejection had again crept into my heart, mind, and spirit. On a day of celebration, I was depressed. As I packed my belongings to return to El Dorado for the summer, I wasn't sure if I wanted to pursue a bachelor's degree. If getting it would make me feel like this, I did not want it.

I had made my share of mistakes during those two years of college, but I had also grown closer to God. I had a different mindset. In some moments, I knew the tests were there to push me towards the will of God. However, other times, I could not discern whether I was headed for the "good, acceptable, and perfect."

. . . .

I had a different mindset. In some moments, I knew the tests were there to push me towards the will of God.

. . . .

Retrospectively, I know Satan was angry. His desire was for me to stop. As a matter of fact, I had already gone too far. Not only was I going beyond what statistics had predicted, but also what he wanted to witness. Wherever you are right now, keep moving. The devil is your personal opponent. His goal is to drive a wedge between you and your aspirations. More importantly, he does not want you to believe in God or yourself. The Bible says he is as a roaring lion seeking who he can devour. *Consider his ways, resist him, and he will flee* (James 4:7).

CHAPTER 11

The College Years - Part II

*"But God's kindness made me what I am, and that
kindness was not wasted on me. Instead,
I worked harder than all the others. It was not
I who did it, but God's kindness was with me."*

— *1 Corinthians 15:10*

I have frequently quoted *I Corinthians 15:10* when people ask the secret of my success. More specifically, when I'm speaking to college-aged youth, I share how much work it takes to finish. Like the Apostle Paul, I worked hard. The summer after graduating from SAU Tech, I had one thing on my mind: transferring to SAU Magnolia. Everything else became less and less important as I realized how close I was to achieving my goals. Due to my estrangement from my parents, I moved in with my oldest sister and sought out employment.

I had learned from the last two years of college that I needed to save money and put it away for hard times. It didn't take long for me to start filling out applications. In a matter of two weeks, I was working. I loved going to work. The earlier I was on the schedule, the better. Nothing had changed; I was at my best in the mornings!

Everything else became less and less important as I realized how close I was to achieving my goals.

Obviously, I did not have a car, but "bumming a ride" was no problem. Customer service was my specialty! When customers would approach the counter, I would smile, compliment them (their clothing, accessories, eyes, etc.), and then ask them if they found everything they needed.

This was what I referred to as my "magic formula" before asking them if they would like to register for an in-store credit card which meant extra pay for me. It worked over and over again. Each time I saw the commission on my paycheck, I knew I had a little more to help me get ready for returning to college. I was on a roll! The only disadvantage was how quickly the end of summer was approaching. When it was near the end, I took a look at the amount I had saved and discovered I was short.

Moving to the university meant I would be staying in the dorms. Thankfully, my tuition and fees were fully covered. However, unfortunately, only a small portion of food services would be included. After contemplating what I would do, I decided I would purchase a mini-refrigerator, microwave, and food items that could be cooked in my dorm room. It was the perfect plan, but an expensive one.

My savings would be gone if I purchased those items. I needed a list of other items including sheets, towels, clothing, etc. This was definitely another roadblock! For days I thought about alternative options, but could not figure out what to do. Then, one day while I was using my "magic formula" on an elderly couple at work, an idea entered my mind. What if they got approved for the credit card? Could I "borrow" their card number (which was retrieved by calling in the request) to purchase the items and then pay their first bill before they knew it? Something told me this was the way! That weekend, I asked a friend for a ride to Little Rock.

I knew I couldn't use the couple's card information locally. My only destination was University Mall. The card could be used at Sears, and the things I needed were definitely there. When I made it to the counter, the sales associate asked me how I would be paying. I told her my "Aunt" gave me her new card number. It could be used temporarily while she was waiting on her permanent card.

Those words entered my mind and rolled off my lips with no effort. I wasn't scared, and I didn't think twice. I left the mall with the microwave, mini-fridge, a pair of boots and a radio. The total was a little over $400.00. I made myself a budget with the intentions of using my next paycheck to call the credit card company and make a payment.

My friend, who provided transportation had no idea of what I had done. Upon returning to El Dorado, I went back to work the next day like nothing had happened. Needless to say, the devil had completely taken over my thoughts and actions.

My next paycheck came about a week later, but I decided to buy a supply of household items, food, and things I needed for my departure soon to my last two years of college. I figured the couple's first statement was at least 30 days away, so I still had time and two more pay periods. Not many days later, when I arrived at work, my boss asked me to come to her office. Two minutes into the conversation, we were both crying. She explained that the couple had called because the credit card company gave them a follow-up call for using their new line of credit for the first time. After a little investigating, everything pointed back to me. I instantly came to my senses!

When she mentioned they were considering pressing charges and that I had committed a felony, I was devastated. I told her my intentions of paying them back before they received their first statement, but that didn't matter. She told me we needed to leave the store immediately. As we were riding in her car, I thought we were on our way to the police station. I was convinced that I was headed to jail or prison. Oddly enough, I was on my way to be convicted of one of the things my biological mom, Marsheill, had been incarcerated for numerous times: theft. I was embarrassed and terrified.

As the car came to a stop, we were sitting in front of a house. She told me the couple was waiting. When I entered their home, the woman looked at me, burst into tears and walked out of the room. Her husband offered us a seat and began to ask me a series of questions. He asked if I had done this before, why I chose them, and how I could so boldly claim that they (an elderly white couple) were my relatives? Each of my answers was brief and followed by an apology. He then explained that my boss had shared my dream of being a teacher. He said with a felony on my record, I would never be able to teach.

The tears that had been building in my eyes began to fall rapidly. He continued by explaining he and his wife were very hurt. Next, he said, "If I report you, you will be in the newspaper. Is that what you want?" I answered, "No." His next statement was totally unexpected. With his voice trembling, he asked, "If I don't report you, will you promise me that one day I will read great things about you in the newspaper?" I was flabbergasted. Fighting back the tears, I said, "Yes, Sir. I promise." With those words, I walked away free with only two stipulations. I would be fired immediately, and my final two paychecks would go directly to the couple. I had literally escaped consequences that I deserved.

In that moment, I thanked God; I was certain He had a plan for my life.

God showed me favor, again. In that moment, I thanked God; I was certain He had a plan for my life. In the next few weeks, a lot of things changed. I truly wanted to pursue what would please God. My faith in Him was increased because He had come to my rescue, much like when I was a little girl. With no job and only a couple of weeks before reporting to Magnolia, I spent a lot of time alone. That was much needed time of isolation, which led to my boyfriend and I ending our relationship. Looking back, I'm certain God knew I did not need the distraction. My mind was clear, and I was ready to finish what I started.

My first day at Southern Arkansas University (SAU) was filled with unpacking and organizing my personal belongings in the freshman dorm, Harrod Hall. My classification was a junior, but since I was new to campus, I was placed there. While moving in, I talked to a Resident's Assistant about how to sign up for that position because I heard they received room and board. I quickly made a mental note and added that to my list of things to do. I was finally beginning the end of my college years.

The general studies were behind me, and now I would engage in coursework specific to my degree plan. I could hardly sleep the night before classes. That morning, I was dressed and exploring the campus before the sun had a chance to come up. Instantly, I fell in love with SAU. The friendly environment and people, as well as the perfectly-sized campus, made everything easily accessible. It was comfortable and fit my description of yet another safe-place. As I dove into child development and early education classes, I found myself handling the content effortlessly.

Academic performance was never an issue because I enjoyed my classes. My only concerns were outside interferences. The familiar burdens of a lack of finances and transportation re-surfaced. A few of my classes required me to do observations at local schools. I was blessed to acquire a few friends who were generous enough to offer to help me handle the obligations. When day-to-day things like money to wash clothes, food, and personal items would get low, I would borrow from friends, make do, or go without.

When my meal account (in the café) was at zero, I found myself hungry on too many occasions to count. Sometimes, friends would invite me to eat out on days when I had no food. On other occasions, I would walk to the nearest service station with minimal coins in hand and scout the store for whatever I could afford. I'm by no means proud of the fact that there were even instances when the girls on my hallway would leave their doors open (talking back and forth) and I would go in and grab food items that were visible. "Stealing to survive" is how I later described my desperate behavior.

I had already learned that it would not come without blood, sweat, and tears so in spite of the obstacles, I was determined.

You might be wondering why I didn't seek out help. Since my parents had only visited me one time at SAU Tech and given me $20 in two years, I knew they weren't a resource that I could depend upon. Jamie (my BFF), my older sister, and some other random acts of kindness had helped to sustain me to this point, and I didn't want to be a burden. Mostly, I felt the responsibility of making my dreams a reality. I had already learned that it would not come without blood, sweat, and tears so in spite of the obstacles, I was determined.

Joining the Genesis Ministry Choir and becoming heavily involved in the on-campus gospel choir was exactly what I needed. Being among a group of young adults who genuinely loved God had a great impact on my life. Rehearsals, singing engagements, and Tuesday night Bible studies (Freedom Rain) provided me with the fuel I needed to stay on track spiritually. After all, I had settled on staying true to my promise to God. The only problem was, when I made a few steps towards righteous living, I would fall back several feet. While I was faithful to the Genesis Ministry and eventually became the president of the choir, I fell into a few temptations.

After the initial invite to go to the club, I said no, but later decided I would go once. That one time turned into more times. I still loved to dance and even began drinking a little again. I would feel so guilty when I would go to choir rehearsal, but convinced myself that no one was perfect. I would simply put on my choir/church face and lift my hands in worship. It was easier than it should have been.

In addition to clubbing and drinking, I became involved with a guy and before long learned I was pregnant. My heart sank! How did I let that happen? What was I thinking? Why me? After a discussion about where life was headed for both of us, he offered to pay for an abortion. Morning sickness plagued me every hour of the day. At the same time, I mulled over whether or not I should end the pregnancy. After falling into a deep depression and missing several classes, I made the decision. We traveled to Little Rock in silence. The building had paintings of red roses on the outside. Roses are usually a symbol of celebration which came across as odd to me. As we drove around back, I thought to myself 'at least no one will see us get out of the car.'

When we entered the clinic, the waiting area was full. I signed in and waited my turn. When I finally looked up and scanned the room, I saw a young lady from El Dorado. I lowered my head, and she did the same. Neither of us looked at one another again. My memory of the time spent in the exam room is blurry, but I can clearly remember one thing. The sound of the equipment was very similar to a vacuum. I was heavily sedated for the procedure, but very conscious shortly afterward. When the nurse entered to issue my discharge, she found me crying. Rubbing my shoulders, she asked if I was in pain and I could only grasp at my heart. I couldn't speak, but I literally felt my heart was breaking.

I had done the unthinkable. Thoughts of ending my life immediately flooded my head. I fought the urge to eject myself from the car every moment of the ride home. The silence in the car was deafening. The young man and I decided what had happened was too difficult to talk about so that was the end of it. And I felt like I didn't deserve to live. For about two weeks, every breath I took physically hurt. When I would start to feel a little better, my thoughts would return to the heinous sin I had committed.

In my mind, I was worse than my biological mother, the woman I despised. At least she had brought me into the world. And on top of all of that, I was a hypocrite. Everyone thought I was the model, young Christian, but I wasn't. The aftermath of this decision put me in a place of shame, guilt, sadness, grief, and despair. The void I felt was unexplainable, and I knew only God could help me because no one else knew.

I carried this heavy burden alone (until my mid-20s), and the devil reminded me of it often. Each time I picked up the phone to call my BFF or thought about sharing with someone else, he would whisper, "Don't do it. They will hate you forever." This pivotal moment introduced me to a level of hopelessness I had never experienced. I was numb to the world, but oddly enough, super-sensitive to God's presence.

I would hide away in my dorm room or by the tree near the pond. Only a few of my friends noticed that I had removed myself from my usual routine (playing dominoes in the "UC" and laughing with the girls). That is what it took for me to give my battered heart over to God fully. Hours and days of crying, praying, facing my demons, and pleading for forgiveness, finally resulted in my releasing some of the pain. I was not completely healed. I knew I had to stay focused. Because of that, I immersed myself in student activities and campus happenings.

Being busy seemed to be the answer to drowning out my negative thoughts and emotions. Within a few months, I became a Resident's Assistant which meant I secured room and board. That was a positive. Finally, I didn't have to worry about where my next meal would come from and whether or not I would have a place to sleep. I also began the process of pledging a sorority and entered a pageant (per a fraternity's request). Most importantly, I sought God harder than I ever had. One night after a gospel concert, several of the choir members and I were talking about how God had met us while we were ministering in song. As we stood underneath a tree, near the Armory, we all began to praise God.

I became overcome with gratefulness as I thought about how He had used me in spite of my recent failures! That evening, I was re-introduced to the feeling that would take over when I sang at Willow Grove as a little girl. However, this time was different! My utterances of thankfulness were soon transformed into unknown tongues. As I spoke, I did not know what I was saying, but a friend standing nearby said, "You are giving thanks to God and only He can comprehend." She had no idea that was my heart's desire. I had longed

> **I became overcome with gratefulness as I thought about how He had used me in spite of my recent failures!**

to be filled with God's spirit! After I did, my path became so much clearer! I attained His forgiveness and forgave myself. I began to flourish in every way after that.

I continued to work diligently as the president of Genesis and even realized I had a crush on one of the musicians, Larry D. Thanks to his brother mentioning the "loud, crunk girl" who was in the choir, he visited the campus choir, Genesis, often. We began to communicate frequently after rehearsals and via the telephone. Immediately, I noticed he was my polar opposite. Larry D. was always reserved while I was more outgoing. He was usually very quiet, and I was the "life of the party."

While I was buzzing around like a social butterfly, he was calmly looking on. As a matter of fact, nearly everything about him, including his family background, was different from me. He was from a two-parent home. His parents had been married since before he was born. He and his family (which consisted of two siblings) were closely knit. Perhaps the most interesting contrast was that his father and mother had been in ministry for many years. In fact, his father had been a pastor since he was twelve years old!

I definitely didn't see that coming! And to top

it all off, he too was an ordained minister. As we spent more and more time getting to know each other, I was glad to have someone to talk to. Larry D. proved to be loyal and a trusted friend. He was an exceptional listener and always a gentleman. But honestly, when the other choir members would make comments about us possibly becoming a couple, I didn't think a guy like him would ever seriously date a girl like me. Around that same time, my first pageant (Miss Black and Gold) which was fully sponsored by the brothers of Alpha Phi Alpha provided me with everything I needed to compete for Miss SAU 1999.

Miss Southern Arkansas University 1999

Talent performance at the Miss Southern Arkansas Pageant.

I had the evening gown, swimsuit, and of course, the natural talent of singing. Why not? I was no beauty queen, but having the last part of my college career paid for by means of a scholarship pageant became my motivation! In the spring of 1999, I entered the Miss Southern Arkansas University pageant. At our first meeting, we were informed that the contest was a preliminary of Miss Arkansas. I was absolutely shocked when I realized it was also an affiliate of the Miss America Foundation. I had watched the pageant many years on television, but I certainly had no desire to be Miss America!

Really, I had no idea what I was getting into, but decided I didn't have anything to lose by trying. As I attended rehearsals for the pageant, I realized I was running against a few very experienced competitors. They wanted to be Miss Arkansas and ultimately, Miss America. That was made very clear when they talked about how they had been contending in pageants since they were toddlers. I was ashamed to tell them my driving force, college funding. On a few occasions, I thought about withdrawing from the competition. The only portion I felt confident about was the talent phase. Thanks to encouragement from friends in my dorm, the Genesis choir, and Larry D., I stayed in the race.

The week before the pageant, I asked my parents if they would attend. They told me they might which meant they would not be there. I wanted their support, but by this time, I was used to not having it. Needless to say, when the day arrived, I was a nervous wreck. Unlike a few of the other girls, I didn't have an entourage. While their personal hairstylists and make-up artists followed them around throughout the day, I was doing the best I could. The interview portion was much easier than I imagined because I loved to talk.

The swimsuit competition was pretty scary because I had never had that much of me exposed in public. My favorite was the talent portion. One of the judges commented that I belted out the jazzy *Show Boat* tune, *"Can't Help Lovin' Dat Man,"* with such a big voice he couldn't believe it came out of my body. At the time I wasn't quite 100 pounds, so I understood his comments. To everyone's surprise and certainly mine, I won Miss Southern Arkansas University 1999! As I stood there to have the crown pinned on my head, I was in total disbelief!

The murmurs from the crowd were a mixture of obvious astonishment from the majority and excitement from my small group of supporters who were in attendance. When it was time for official photos, on either side of me stood the first and second runner-ups. The two young ladies had trained extensively for the title well before I decided to compete a few weeks before. For one of the first times in my life, I was speechless! That night, I sat on my dorm room bed with a beautiful crown on my head and a folder in my hand which was full of complimentary prizes and a letter stating that my tuition was paid for the next (my final) school year! God had once again proven His unfailing love and undeniable power!

That same night, I received a call from a writer with the Magnolia newspaper. After congratulating me, he asked, "How does it feel to be the first African American to win the title of Miss SAU after 90 years?" I had no idea I was the first. No one had brought that to my attention. Being that I had always been a lover of all people, I had not even considered the issue of race. Put simply, I was honored, humbled and I couldn't believe this was happening to me! The next morning, a friend brought me the newspaper, and I was on the front page!

Someone else called to tell me I was on the front page in El Dorado too! The headline read "Curley: First Black Miss SAU." My first thoughts went straightway to the couple who had spared me after my poor decisions. The gentleman had mentioned that he wanted to see me in the paper for good reasons. With God's help, that had happened. My tears flowed as I gave God praise for His wonderful grace and mercy! The next few weeks went by rapidly with additional interviews, preparing for Miss Arkansas, and fulfilling my duties as Miss SAU.

In the midst of the excitement, Larry D. had become one of my closest confidants. He also became my first and only boyfriend while attending SAU. The joke among some of the Genesis choir members was that he finally decided to make it official when I became Miss SAU. That was not the case, but it was funny! After our first date at Western Sizzlin, I returned to Harrod Hall and told my friends we would one day be married. They knew I had never dated anyone at SAU, so they were shocked and told me to slow down.

Somehow, I just knew he was the one. The more time we spent together, the more I loved him. In my mind, we had established a rapport I had never experienced with anyone else, and I knew he felt the same way. The invitation to meet his parents meant things were getting serious. He said he wanted his family to get to know me. I was open to that and looked forward to being in a family-oriented environment. On my first visit to their home, I felt welcomed, but also a little uncomfortable. After all, I was the oldest son's new girlfriend. The feelings of uneasiness were bearable because Larry D. always made me feel special. In fact, God knew I needed his unwavering support and encouragement. During what should have been one of the happiest times in my college career, adversity came in like a flood.

When I went home to share the news of Miss SAU with my parents, I took some of the flowers that I acquired to my mom. She loved plants and flowers, so I thought it would be a nice gesture. Somehow, the conversation escalated, and I was accused of bragging about my winnings. It ended with me being told that I could have shared some of the money that I won. I tried to explain, but they didn't understand my winnings were either in the form of scholarships or gift certificates. I never mentioned being Miss SAU to my parents again.

Back on campus, rejection came in another form. As I began prepping for Miss Arkansas, I sought out help from the organizers of Miss SAU. After no response to my emails and calls, I was informed that the pageant coordinators had resigned. I explained that I needed help because I had never done anything like this before, but no one stepped up. I was naive at first, but then it all began to make sense. It was a hard pill to swallow, but the resistance was coming because of the color of my skin.

A few people had called it to my attention, but I didn't want to believe it. When I entered a couple of downtown Magnolia boutiques to use gift certificates that I had been awarded, it became apparent. One store clerk said, "The half-off items are in the back of the store," as soon as I entered. She did this without looking up and never acknowledged me again. When I requested information about whether a dress could be ordered in my size, I was told size 2/4 was "not normal." Her condescending tone and patronizing facial expression hurt my feelings and angered me.

After a similar encounter in another shop, I almost resolved to throw away the gift certificates. It was clear several people were not pleased with me representing "their" community. The negative feelings of not being accepted reemerged and I found myself once again "Living Rejected." Luckily for me, I had a diverse group of friends. I deduced the only way I would be able to receive good customer service was if I asked a couple of my white friends to help me select my wardrobe for Miss Arkansas.

Initially, I didn't reveal why I invited them.

Their presence resulted in a completely different response (from the same associate mentioned above); it was demoralizing, but my reality. Conversely, the black community from the surrounding areas came to my aid. It was amazing how sponsorship came from people I had never met. Strangers collected financial donations, secured hair and make-up services, obtained a photographer for my headshots, provided professional production of my instrumental music, and organized limousine transportation to Miss Arkansas. All of these things came without solicitation. I was invited to numerous events and recognized as "someone the (black) community should celebrate."

It wasn't necessarily how I wanted to be viewed, but yet a comforting feeling. I would not have been prepared for the Miss Arkansas pageant without the kind efforts of so many arbitrary displays of compassion. As the semester came to an end and the summer was approaching, I faced another challenge. I needed a place to live (in Magnolia) to continue grooming for Miss Arkansas and attend summer school.

When the dorms closed, I was homeless. Thankfully, I had a close friend, Eric (who had 3 other roommates), who was renting a house a few miles from the college. Very few people knew that in the months leading up to the Miss Arkansas 1999 pageant, Miss SAU was sleeping on a friend's bedroom floor. It wasn't the best case scenario, but there wasn't a day I didn't give God thanks for that uncomfortable egg crate mattress pad!

Being a Miss Arkansas participant was completely out of my element! Staying in a fancy hotel, eating delicate foods, and being surrounded by "beauty queens" was not my norm. I was like Dorothy in the Wizard of Oz. I definitely wasn't in "Kansas" anymore. That week was full, but fun! The rehearsals, fierce competitors, and my lack of experience were a little overwhelming. Reading my Bible and daily love letters from Larry D. (which I still have) made things much easier! Throughout the week, several people came to watch me compete.

Friday's phase of the pageant, talent night, brought my largest crowd. At the end of the night, we entered a large room to greet our supporters; I was relieved to see my people, family, and friends. The biggest shock was my biological mother's surprise appearance! That was the first time I had seen her since I was a toddler, but I knew it was her.

Our encounter was extremely brief, but enough to stir up emotions I did not want to contend with. Looking at her was like looking in the mirror. That in itself was enough to deal with. With the room so full of people, I knew I had to hold myself together. It took a lot of effort, but I made the conscious decision to deal with those emotions later. Saturday would be the final night of the pageant, and I could not allow myself to become distracted.

On closing night, I was overtaken with gratefulness, as several of the young ladies I had formed bonds with asked me to lead us in prayer. While some of the contestants had opted to be completely engrossed in the competition, some of us had taken the opportunity to become acquainted and celebrate each other's accomplishments. That night, I was honored to be awarded another scholarship: the "Best All-Around First Timer Award!"

Clearly, I didn't win Miss Arkansas, but I had another remarkable blessing behind me. Thanks to God's intentional plan, I had my final year of college (already paid in full) ahead of me. The fall semester introduced an easy class load. With scholarships taking care of my tuition and fees, my Pell Grant refund was more than it had ever been. This made my decision to pledge a sorority my next goal. After successfully making it through the rush process, Alpha Kappa Alpha (AKA) was my choice.

The three principles of the sorority: Sisterhood, Scholarship, and Service to All Humankind were an excellent fit. The signature colors, pink and green were two of my favorites, and pretty girls wearing pearls was appealing! I had many late nights filled with fun and excitement with my line sisters. We were all different but formed a love for each other that added to my list of people who I will always cherish.

I had also become involved in the church where Larry D.'s father pastored. The church was in Emerson, about twenty miles from SAU. Almost every time I visited, I was announced as "Miss SAU" and the young lady who Larry D. was dating. The congregation was very welcoming, and I absolutely loved their youth and young adult ministries. After visiting several times, I made Roadside Church of God in Christ my new church home.

In December of 1999, my line sisters and I came "off line" and "crossed," which means we completed the initiation process to become members of AKA. Three days later, Larry D. invited me to dinner to celebrate me getting my letters. I wore a beautiful green sweater to commemorate my accomplishment. We ate dinner at La Barron's restaurant in a candlelit room. Oddly enough, we were the only two people in the room.

After dinner, when I stood up to exit the room, Larry D. stood in front of me, softly put his hands on my shoulders, and helped me to sit back down. In what seemed like one motion, he kneeled down on one knee, removed a ring box from his jacket pocket and began telling me he wanted us to spend the rest of our lives together.

. . . .

In what seemed like one motion, he kneeled down on one knee, removed a ring box from his jacket pocket and began telling me he wanted us to spend the rest of our lives together.

. . . .

After eight short months of dating, we became engaged! I later learned that he had visited the restaurant earlier in the day and made arrangements for the proposal. Due to my estrangement from my parents, I also had no idea he had respectfully asked for my hand in marriage. When we left La Barron's, we made a couple of stops before returning to SAU. Everyone was excited for us, but no one was happier than we were! Honestly, the rest of that semester went by very quickly. That's probably because I felt like I was floating on cloud nine!

CHAPTER 12

Momentous Occasions

"I will bless the Lord at all times;
His praise shall continually be in my mouth."

— Psalm 34:1

"Bless the Lord at all times," is a phrase that carries a lot of meaning. When David wrote this popular Psalm, he was on the run from King Saul. In fact, he went in hiding and later pretended to be "crazy" in order to escape being killed. However, it was impossible for him to get away from the favor that was in his life. In spite of Saul's jealousy, God had a designated purpose for David's life.

He went through a lot of momentous occasions to get there, but in the end, he became the king and fulfilled his destiny. The word "momentous" is an adjective with a number of alternatives listed in the thesaurus. A few that describe the timeline presented below are: significant, crucial, vital, meaningful, and historic.

2000

Early 2000, I continued my studies and started planning our wedding. I was 21, and Larry D. was 23. We were young, but eager to be married and start our new lives together. Neither of us knew how much work we were in for! A decorator/caterer who attended our church, my BFF, Jamie, and one of my high school mentors were life-savers! I'm sorry to say, my parents were not willing to do the traditional part of the bride's parents. The wedding of my dreams (which happened to be pretty simple) was fully our responsibility.

In fact, with me as a full-time student, Larry D. worked countless hours to make sure everything was covered financially. The only thing my parents promised to do was to take care of my wedding dress. But when the day came to choose the dress, my mom was a no-show. I called to ask her if she was coming and she told me to pick it out and let her know how much I needed. That was a hard day. Truthfully, I chose a dress that was deemed "appropriate" for marrying a minister, the pastor's son. It wasn't what I wanted, but I didn't want to be disrespectful. Reluctantly, I said "yes to the dress" and was able to cover the down payment with Pell Grant funds.

Honestly, as time passed, I wasn't sure if my mom and dad would attend the ceremony. I came to a hard decision. If I had to, I would walk down the aisle alone. Larry D. had the sweet suggestion of reaching out to my biological father, Charley Roy. After some discussion, we sent an invitation giving him the opportunity to attend. I had only talked to my father a few times, but definitely longed for a relationship. Marsheill, my biological mom, was incarcerated at the time. In spite of the ups and downs with family-related issues, the wedding planning had to continue.

My OCD tendencies came in handy as I began to write every single detail in a spiral notebook titled, "Our Wedding Day." A month before the nuptials, the congregation celebrated the opening of another sanctuary located across the street. Our big day would be the first event held in the newly constructed Greater Roadside C.O.G.I.C. The color of the pews, a deep purple, would perfectly compliment my purple and lavender wedding decor. Two weeks before the wedding, the dress shop called. Only a few minor alterations were needed, and the remaining balance was due.

Our Wedding Day!

I was appalled to learn that my parents weren't sending the funds! My first thought was no dress, no wedding. I was devastated. Larry D. said it would work out, but I knew it wasn't right for him to pay for my dress. Have you ever heard the expression "ram in the bush?" If not, Genesis 22 is where it originated. God provided for Abraham just in the nick of time. Jamie's parents, Mr. and Mrs. Benton, wrote the check to cover the remaining balance on my wedding dress! I had always considered them as a set of bonus parents, but from that day, I never addressed them otherwise, my Mom and Dad Benton! With that speed bump crossed, the other arrangements fell in place. On May 20, 2000, we had the most beautiful wedding!

The church was filled to capacity, all of the music was top-notch, and the décor was perfect. Of course, like any other bride, there were small details that I'd like to forget (i.e., people arriving late, my mother wearing a white dress, a surprise limo that ended up taking us away from our reception/ guests, etc.), but all in all, it was superbly special! One interesting memory from that day was a gentleman approaching me while we were greeting guests. He tapped me on the shoulder and said, "Do you know who I am?" My heart literally skipped a few beats!

Was this Charley Roy, my father? Did he come to celebrate one of the most important days of my life with me? I had only laid eyes on him for about five minutes (in a very dark room) a few years before. I didn't know what he looked like. When I finally replied with a soft, "No," he said, "I'm your new uncle, Larry D.'s great uncle." I smiled, hugged him and thanked him for coming. Every time I see him, I remember the moment we first met and how I thought he was my father.

In that moment, the uncertainty of who I was and where I came from had the potential to ruin our day, but instead, I wiped the tears away and chose to be happy! The day ended with a limo dropping us off at our new address: 701 Gladys St., Magnolia, Arkansas. Larry D. had not only been working to pay for a wedding, but also had fully prepared a home for us. The four-room (kitchen/living room, bathroom, and 2 bedrooms) house was a rental property that belonged to a member of our church. Many times we have reflected on how when the wind blew, the curtains in the house would rise. Nonetheless, it was our first home, and we were

> **In that moment, the uncertainty of who I was and where I came from had the potential to ruin our day, but instead, I wiped the tears away and chose to be happy!**

content. Our life as a married couple had begun. Every day was not perfect, but we were certainly enjoying marital bliss!

As I began my last semester of college and student teaching, Larry D. continued to work. Every weekend, we would pack a bag and leave town. We loved to travel and spend quality time together. Texarkana was one of our favorite places to go. We would visit our friends, Corey and Teresa, and get back in time for Sunday morning services. Larry D. was an intricate part of the church where his father served as pastor. He played the organ, preached occasionally, assisted with the youth ministry, and did whatever was needed to make things go smoothly. I admired his Christian commitment and did my best to complement his efforts.

Primarily, I sang in the choir and offered the musical selection during the Call to Discipleship. It did not take long before I knew my main role was to smile, be compliant, and stay clear of anything that might make me a target for confusion. I was not a "P.K.," a Preacher's Kid, but I was married to one. That in itself was a lot to handle. Although we both were challenged on many occasions, we were faithful to the church and our spiritual leaders, his parents. We had some responsibilities within the ministry and tried our best to serve with a smile. That was not easy and certainly demanded a lot of our time.

It was a sacrifice, to say the least. At last, in December, I completed all of the requirements to graduate college! I was about to cross the finish line. My dream had finally come to fruition. Much like Joseph in the Bible, God had shown me what was to come, however, He had opted to leave out the details. In his dream, Joseph saw himself in a position of authority with everyone bowing down to him. What he didn't see was himself being thrown into the pit, being plagued with haters, or his placement in prison. After all of that, he was promoted to the palace (Genesis 37, 39, 40-4). I believe if I had known the struggle to get to my "palace" (graduating college), it's likely that I would have never started. I'm so thankful God saw my ending at the beginning. He gave me the grace to get through it.

Not only did I graduate, but I had passed the dreaded Praxis exams (after a few attempts on the math portion), applied for a teacher's license and started applying for jobs. I opted to walk in May of 2001, but my dream of being a teacher was finally about to be a reality! In fact, it was the perfect Christmas present! We had no idea we were about to add to the excitement of me entering my career. First comes love, then comes marriage, here comes P.J. with a baby carriage! Somewhere around our sixth month of marriage (November), we had conceived, and I was pregnant! It wasn't our intention to have a baby so soon, but God had other plans. For nearly 24 hours a day, I battled morning sickness. I could barely sit up in bed or step outside without vomiting.

I still don't know how I survived the job interviews for teaching positions in the El Dorado School District. I was already nervous about the scarcity of positions for half of a school-year, but I wanted to start as soon as possible. That December, I applied and was offered two different teaching opportunities. I chose fifth grade at Northwest Elementary. Over the Christmas break, I visited the empty classroom and envisioned myself standing in front of a group of young minds.

With my lesson plan book and four or five textbooks in hand, I walked out ready to prepare for my first semester of teaching. I couldn't believe it! I was a teacher and a soon-to-be mother too! These facts hugely resonated with me. As I was carrying my own child in my womb, I would be taking on the responsibility of teaching, molding, and loving other people's children.

2001

The first full week of January, I started teaching 5th grade. I commuted with a friend from Magnolia. Larry D. used our vehicle to get back and forth to work. The morning sickness was better, but still an adjustment. The staff at Northwest immediately showed compassion for me as a new teacher and an expecting mom. They obviously knew I would need their support.

Several times a day I would have to ask students to leave my classroom and visit the principal. My school days were filled with constant re-direction, and honestly, I did more correcting than teaching. At first, I thought it was because I was a new teacher, "fresh meat" to the oldest children in the school. I later learned that the bulk of my class had a history of undesirable behaviors.

A few of my co-workers believed other grade-level teachers had specifically avoided the children. This resulted in a room filled with tough kids from various backgrounds. Most of them were from poverty stricken homes and had difficult home environments. I could relate to them and somehow found a way with the wayward ones.

It was not easy, but I decided I wanted to make

a difference in their lives. And with my motto of always being "firm, friendly, and fair," I survived that one semester of teaching 5th grade. I will admit it was the toughest group of kids I've ever encountered to date. I was cursed, threatened, and disrespected daily. There were days when I wanted to quit and hardly a day went by that I didn't cry.

Some days, Larry D. would drive me to work and spend the day with me. A few times, he stepped in to assist; he literally chased one of my students when he tried to leave the building. My building principal would check on me throughout the day and was always very encouraging. She told me, "If you can make it through this semester, you will be one of the best in our profession." I had to remind myself of her words almost every morning.

In May of that year, I was scheduled to "walk" at SAU, Magnolia! I decided against a December graduation because I wanted the full experience. I remember trying on my cap and gown several times because I was six months pregnant. Life was grand! I was expecting a child with my wonderful husband, working in a profession I had always loved, and at last, crossing my Bachelor's Degree off of my list! I sent invitations to a long list of family and friends.

Gray skies and a chance of rain on graduation day did not take away from my excitement! Graduating with high honors was an accomplishment I had earned, and I wanted to enjoy the momentous affair. Like everyone else, I was eager to look for family and friends in the crowd when it was over. My biggest supporters, Larry D. and Jamie, were right there with big hugs and smiles! It wasn't long before I got the news that my parents and sisters were not in attendance. Although my mouth said, "It's okay," my heart was destroyed.

The tears were already flowing from happiness, so the ones added due to disappointment were easily disguised. Each time I thought I had beaten the debilitating effect of rejection, it would visit again. Rejection was an unwanted guest and always stayed longer than I expected. I'm sure being pregnant only added to my emotional state. As I began to visit the obstetrician on a more regular basis, he would always ask if I was stressed. My blood pressure was high, and the baby's heartbeat was fast. I

> **The tears were already flowing from happiness, so the ones added due to disappointment were easily disguised.**

explained that I was a teacher and he took that as my answer. Truthfully, I didn't feel good most of the time. I still had some morning sickness and felt drained by the end of the day. When the school year ended, I was glad to see my first summer break!

Early in the summer, we moved to El Dorado. Three weeks before my due date, I began having significant pains. Initially, I was told that they were Braxton Hicks contractions. As they progressively worsened, I was hospitalized for observation. My husband and I were naturally concerned. After giving me medication to avoid pre-term labor, I was sent home after spending a few days in the hospital. At that point, we contacted our families and told them to be on standby.

Our excitement was building! Jamie and a host of friends had me an enormous Baby Shower. At the shower, Larry D.'s present was a cute baby bag with the name "Lance: God's Helper" embroidered on it. With a lot of rest, I managed to almost make it to my due date. Our lives changed forever when Larry DaKeith Yarbrough, Jr. (L.J.) was born on August 9, 2001! The moment we laid eyes on him, his resemblance to his father was unmistakable. We both laughed about ordering another baby bag.

This one would read "Larry: Victorious One." We happily received visitors at both the hospital and our new apartment. L.J. was my in-law's first grandchild. Needless to say, he had all of the attention! Larry D. called to announce our son's birth, but neither of my parents came to visit. Sadly, our estrangement had grown to the point that we hardly ever spoke.

The love I had for my baby was entirely different from anything I had ever felt.

By now, I think I've established that I'm an emotional being. Motherhood magnified that to an astronomical degree. I was terrified, joyful, elated, overwhelmed, and unprepared. I knew the basics from closely watching my sisters with their children and babysitting, but I was officially a parent, a mother. The love I had for my baby was entirely different from anything I had ever felt.

Even when I was tired from the sleepless nights and I felt inadequate, loving L.J. came easy! I wanted to be perfect because he was perfect. I questioned myself with every move while also teaching Larry D., Sr. everything I knew. He was so careful with his namesake and always a huge help. Since L.J.

was born the week prior to school starting, I did not get a chance to start my next teaching assignment as a second-grade teacher from the beginning of the school year.

I wanted to be there, but I wanted nothing more than to be with L.J. 24 hours a day, whether I was sleep deprived, an emotional wreck, or going through the cycle of breastfeeding and changing diapers, I knew my love for him would prevail. It was in those moments that my head and heart could not make the connection. How was my biological mother able to stay away from me for the past 16 years? The more I tried not to think about that fact, the more I did.

The frequency of these thoughts led me to something that a lot of women deal with, Postpartum Depression. I was functioning (sluggishly) and smiling through motherhood, but my inner being was anxious, sad, detached, and extremely fearful. When L.J. would cry or become fussy, I would feel incompetent. When more milk or a dry diaper didn't soothe him, I immediately felt as if I wasn't sufficiently capable of caring for him. My doctor told me the feelings were normal, but I didn't feel right. As I prepared to return to work, I found myself feeling a little guilty because

I was thankful for the break from motherly duties and the reoccurring depressive episodes.

Teaching second grade brought me a great deal of joy. The 2001-2002 school year, my husband and I worked together. He was employed as a mentor. I was so glad to have him nearby. Surprisingly, all of sudden, I no longer felt like a confident teacher. For lack of better words, I wasn't sure if I could trust myself. I continued to teach with a passion, but it took a great deal of effort. A veteran teacher across the hall, Mrs. Virginia McDaniel, became my mentor, friend, and "big sister."

Although she had taught for nearly thirty years, she never looked down on me or doubted my ability. In fact, she encouraged me weekly to keep working hard and go beyond classroom teaching. She had no idea I was struggling to come to work every day. Postpartum had settled on my shoulders, and there was no sign of the pressure being released! When I wanted to quit, Mrs. McDaniel and my model 2nd-grade students made me look forward to each school day. God certainly knows who to put in your path and when.

In October, I received a call that my mom (Ernestine) was in the hospital. I reluctantly went to visit. When we arrived in the room, I purposely had L.J.'s baby carrier facing me. I asked how she was and found out she had a heart attack. As I was getting the details about her treatment plan, she said, "Turn the baby around and let me see him." That was her first time to lay eyes on L.J. He was almost three months old. I positioned his carrier on her hospital bed and fought back tears.

What if she had not been in the hospital? When would she have met our baby? This, like most things those days, sent me into a three or four day downward spiral. After work every day, I would pick up the baby and go straight to bed. I would only get up if he needed something. On many nights, I did not cook dinner or talk to Larry D. I had lost control of coping with the weight of my intense emotions. On Wednesdays and Sundays, I would pull myself together and put on my church face. Church in many ways was a sedative for me.

. . . .

I had lost control of coping with the weight of my intense emotions.

. . . .

When in worship, the cloud would seem to move from over my head. The moment we were in the car driving back from Emerson to El Dorado, the cloud would return. I thought I could hold it together, but one day, finally, my true emotional state was revealed at school, in my classroom. As I was writing on the whiteboard, I turned to ask my students a question and couldn't form the words. I turned back to try again, and everything went black. I woke up in the emergency room with the worst headache I had ever experienced.

I was told later that I fainted. A student, Michael, went across the hall to get Mrs. McDaniel. She then called the ambulance. The doctors treated me for one of my first migraine headaches and told me to take a couple of days off work. After a few days of rest, I made it through the rest of the semester. Our first holiday season as a family of three was very special, but also a pivotal moment for me. Holidays had always been difficult, but were no longer about my happiness. L.J. was the new focus.

Larry D. and I always spent Thanksgiving in Louisiana with his mother's family and Christmas with my family. Both holidays were memorable because he was the newest addition to both sides of the family. After the stressful holidays, I longed for some downtime. Most people didn't realize I was (and still am) an outgoing introvert. I'm definitely the life of the party – until I'm home. During that time (and honestly many times now), the sooner

I could be alone, the better. During that season of life, the re-charge process, unfortunately, took longer than usual. So much so that Larry D. and I were growing apart.

Put simply, I was not easy to live with. I was extremely moody and confrontational. He was so patient, but obviously irritated with my ups and downs. I can't imagine what it was like to live with me. On my lowest days, he was my rock. Neither of us liked where I was or what I was going through, and unfortunately, we had not seen our worst day.

2002

Ironically, one Sunday afternoon, after attending church, that day arrived. Before sharing the details, I'll admit, parts of that day are blurry. I asked my husband to help me with the details to ensure accuracy. Immediately after worship, I overheard a few people discussing me (harsh, negative accusations). A visiting minister had already exposed the congregation by publicly declaring, "You're the Pastor's daughter-in-law, and they surely don't like you." This was not a surprise to me because I had been bullied and treated badly.

I remained quiet to "keep the peace," but on that occasion, I became furious. Once we were in the car, I told Larry D. I was not going back to the church. He asked me to calm down, and my mind said, "He's on their side." L.J. and I were in the backseat. Thankfully, he was asleep. To say "I lost it" is an understatement. The entire ride home (40 miles), I screamed, beat the car windows and the back of the seats and tried to open the car door several times. Larry continued to drive, talk calmly, and pray out loud. Nothing calmed me down.

Satan completely took residence in my mind; he came in like a flood and snatched my sanity. When we arrived at the apartment, I ran into the house and began packing bags. I had decided to leave Larry D. and L.J. I told him they would be better off without me, and that was what "they" wanted anyway. He was trying to console me, but it wasn't working.

After he convinced me to stop packing, I told him I would stay, but I wanted to die. I sat on the bed and wrote a letter to my three sisters. I shared in a few words how I was in too much pain to live any longer. Then I decided to leave again. When Larry D. would not allow me to exit the apartment, I ran in the bathroom and locked the door.

I started searching for something to harm myself. Rambling through drawers and cabinets, I found a razor and began trying to cut myself. Praise God, I was unsuccessful. Right before I was able to try for the third time, Larry D. pried the door open. When he did, I grabbed a coat, scarf, and gloves and ran out of the apartment. It was a sunny, March day! Strangely enough, I was dressed for cold weather. I was definitely not thinking straight. I started walking as fast as I could. I don't know where I was going. I walked and walked.

About 45 minutes later, I noticed a police car following me. The officer pulled up beside me and asked if I was Shaneil Yarbrough. I said, "Yes." He said my husband was concerned and that I should head home. I told him no. He said I was a danger to myself and possibly others. My choices were to either go home or be put in his police car. That was a sobering moment. Considering my biological mother's history with the law, I knew I didn't want that. As I walked back home, he slowly drove behind me. Once there, I stormed in upset because my husband had called the police.

I found Larry D. inside with his parents and L.J. He was awake at this point, but had been asleep through the entire episode. That was without a doubt God's doing! I went to my bedroom and listened as the police officer gave some suggestions about getting me some help. My in-laws, my pastor and his wife, offered prayer and I said I didn't want it. I told them God didn't love me and they didn't either.

I asked them to leave me alone, and they did. When I walked into the living room, I saw them comforting Larry D. as he sat on the floor crying, but I wasn't phased by it. When he stood up, he told me I needed to go to the hospital. I resisted initially, but later agreed. My in-laws took L.J., and in the pit of my stomach, I thought I'd never see him again. Once at the hospital, all of the weird and uncomfortable feelings came to the surface again. I felt as if everyone was looking at me and that police officers were on standby to take me away.

It was only a figment of my imagination. When I underwent a psychological evaluation, and my husband answered questions, the doctor gave me two options: (1) be admitted to a Behavioral Health Unit or (2) go to ICU and be placed in a straitjacket. I didn't like either choice. He named locations in Little Rock. I quickly said no because my sisters lived there and I didn't want them to know. We decided on the Behavioral Health Unit of Glenwood Regional Medical Center in Monroe, LA.

By this time, it was very late in the evening. After packing a bag, Larry D. and his father transported me there.

We arrived in the middle of the night and entered into a very quiet hallway. Following the admission's paperwork, Larry D. and I briefly hugged, and I watched the large, metal doors lock behind him. I spent the next hour having all of my personal belongings checked in and were only issued appropriate items for my room. Most of my personal items were confiscated: shoestrings, belts, etc. Hygiene products (including toothpaste) had to be checked out, used, and returned. The nurse took me into a small room to get my vitals, and I accidentally saw myself in the mirror.

Who was that person? I looked terrible, beaten down, and despondent. I lowered my head, staring catatonically at the floor. The nurse said, "No, look up! You can be like this forever or you can accept this treatment and get better." She ended our time together by taking my photo and escorting me to an empty room. That room was a replica of a TV psychiatric ward. The walls were white and were soft (padded). The bedding was white. The furniture (bed, chest of drawers, and nightstand) were white. It was a complete white-out. A small bathroom had another door that was locked. I wondered who or what was on the other side. I buzzed the desk to ask if someone else was on the other side and was told yes. She instructed me to lock my door and knock before entering the bathroom. I was terrified.

What would I do if the person came in my room? At that moment, I decided I was not going to sleep. I sat on the bed. Before long, I was pacing through the room. Thoughts were running through my head, "I hate myself... I'm my mother's child... I've abandoned my child, and he'll never forgive me... Larry D. will leave me... I am so unstable and broken." At that moment, as my breath seemed to be escaping my body, I was searching for anything to get me through the night. I opened the chest of drawers to put away my handful of items. When I looked in the last drawer, a blue Bible was staring back at me. There He (God) was – a present help in the time of trouble (Psalm 46:1).

At that moment, as my breath seemed to be escaping my body, I was searching for anything to get me through the night.

The first scripture I opened to was Psalm 40:1-3, *"I waited patiently for the Lord; He turned to me and heard my cry. He lifted me out of the horrible pit, out of the miry clay, and set my feet upon a rock, and established my goings. He put a new song in my mouth, even praise unto our God: many shall see it, and fear, and shall trust in the Lord."* At that moment, I didn't have any other choice but to be patient. I knew I was in a horrible pit, sinking sand. What I had mistaken for my rock(s) (my biological parents, adoptive parents, family members, friends, and even my husband and son) were not the answer.

God was my rock, and only He could set me on the right path after this. I wanted so badly to sing a new tune and allow Him to get the glory. What I didn't know is what the next day, week, months, and years would hold. Thankfully, I knew who was holding me. I fell asleep for a brief time before being buzzed to wake up for morning vitals.

I sheepishly walked out of the room in my pajamas eager to see what this place was like during the daytime. I immediately encountered several people in the hallway. Guess what? They all looked "normal." Breakfast was offered, but I didn't have an appetite. During the morning unexpected medication administration, the nurse insisted that I drink some juice. The first several hours, I was assessed thoroughly. The doctors and therapist completed their evaluations and asked a lot of questions.

When that was over, I didn't waste any time asking for a diagnosis. I was told that I had a mental illness, manic depression. Manic depression (now known as Bipolar Disorder) explained what I had always called my ups and downs. My suicidal thoughts, persistent depressed mood, and the sudden disinterest in life's activities were determining symptoms. I told them about the days that I would laugh until my belly hurt and other days when I didn't want to get out of bed. I described how sometimes, I didn't have the energy to lift my head. There had even been times when I found myself going several days without speaking. I would cry for hours.

As attentive to my appearance as I had always been, there were even some days that I didn't take a shower. Hearing all of this, I was immediately put on a regiment of medications to test out "what would work best." I realized all of the patients were taking a lot of medicine when a couple of them asked me what was in my "drug cocktail."

218 | Shaneil "PJ" Yarbrough

The staff eased me into the structured schedule on my first day, and I ended the day by speaking briefly to Larry D. by phone. I'd like to say it was only an overnight stay with a next-day discharge, but it wasn't.

Every day there was the same. Morning vitals, breakfast, medication, individual therapy, free time, group therapy, lunch, afternoon medication, cool-down time, family visits, more therapy, dinner, evening medication, and bedtime. Some of the residents were comatose while others were very talkative. Oddly enough, I made friends. Cindy and Greg were much older than me and had very different stories, but we connected instantly. We would read our Bibles together during free-time. They both said I was like an angel sent there to help them. I felt the same about them.

In our group sessions, I was shocked to find out that there were a variety of professionals including a dentist, a pastor, drug addicts, and all in all, "normal people." As we shared what led to our admission into the program, we would joke about being in the insane asylum. One of the doctor's suggested that we practice seeing things the way that people "on the outside" would see us. He told us we were scarred when we walked in, but this scar would be one of the most visible, for the rest of our lives.

I explained my roles as a wife, mom, teacher, and minister's wife, and how I was unsure if I could function again. I quickly realized everyone else had the same fears. Life had browbeaten us to the point that we couldn't imagine things ever being different. The staff was very reassuring. Each session provided us with coping skills, strategies for getting through tough times, and a variety of techniques that we began using immediately.

Day 2, Larry D. came to Monroe (a 3-hour round trip) to visit me for one hour. He continued these visits on a daily basis until I was discharged. I was glad to see him, but I didn't understand why he came. I thought he would walk away and join the people who rejected me, but he didn't. He was working, taking care of L.J. (our six-month-old baby) and being a faithful, supportive husband. When he could have walked away, he stayed. He took his wedding vows seriously; the good and the bad, in sickness and in health. I was sick: mentally, emotionally, spiritually, and even physically.

I was in desperate need of restoration. One therapy session that I attended sticks out in my memory. It was a therapeutic art session. The instructor told us to draw an outdoor scene of our choice. I drew a sun in the sky with a few clouds and a large tree with a hole in the middle and jagged tree bark. I finished the drawing by adding five flowers in the green grass (two on one side and three on the other) at the bottom of the page.

As we debriefed, the therapist told me that I wanted the sun to shine, but clouds were always looming in my life. Accurate. He said the large tree was my life and the squirrel's hole was a representation of the many voids that needed to be filled. I immediately burst into tears! He said the green grass was proof that I had some type of positive foundation, more than likely, spiritually. Even though I was angry with God, that seemed to pretty much be on target. Lastly, he said the five flowers depicted 5 special individuals (more than likely family members) in my life who I held close to my heart.

I identified those as Larry D., L.J., Latosha, LaTreace, and Ashley (my three sisters). My sisters and I were all adults with separate lives, but the bond that had been secured through our adoption was intact. There were times we were distant, but (like now) when we get together, what we share is apparent. Needless to say, that art session opened the door to so many conversations. I was asked a lot of hard questions, but felt so much better after digging deeper into my history. As we worked through multiple therapy sessions, I realized that God had me there for a reason.

> **I was asked a lot of hard questions, but felt so much better after digging deeper into my history.**

My time at the Behavioral Health Unit (often referred to as the mental hospital or crazy house) was a pivotal point in my life. After some days in intense therapy, taking a lot of medication, and riding an emotional roller-coaster, my doctors and therapists started discussing life outside of the facility. Immediately, my heart and mind were flooded with questions. Could I return to my life as a wife, mother, and teacher? Would I be able to pick up where I left off? Did I want to go back to church?

If people found out where I had been, how would they treat me? I felt a great deal of uneasiness on my last day at Glenwood. A part of me was not sure if I could function in the real world. There was a sense of safety and security knowing that I didn't have the responsibilities of life. Besides, the medication was doing the work for me. Could

I continue with all of my new restrictions and successfully navigate life? I was about to find out. I was released from the facility, and it was not on a weekend pass! With God's help, I never returned. The ride home with Larry D. was awkward, but refreshing.

I know he was concerned about me because he was overly compensating at my every move. He had always been a gentleman, but I noticed that he was treating me as if I was a fragile piece of glass. In fact, it was as if I was a glass that had just freshly been glued back together. I was scheduled to return to work soon. However, the priority was to secure a therapist and ensure that my medication was prescribed locally.

The moment I pulled into the parking lot and walked into South Arkansas Regional Health Center, I felt like all eyes were on me. I was convinced that someone would see me and tell my principal that I was a patient there. I would walk fast to get in, sit in the corner of the waiting room with my back to the door and drive off quickly at the end of my weekly visits. As far as I knew, other than my husband, his family, and my co-worker, Mrs. McDaniel, no one knew where I had been or what I had been through. It was my secret! I couldn't bear to bring that kind of embarrassment to Larry D., my family, friends, or my career. Keeping all of that inside while taking one pill to get up, one pill to get through the day, and another one to fall asleep definitely took its toll on me.

For the most part, I was managing life pretty well, but I had a long way to go. Being home with my husband and baby was comforting. Returning to work was more or less a seamless transition. At that point, church was a part of the routine, so I attended, but stayed to myself. My therapist told me to take my time and let life happen naturally. It was an uphill journey. There were days when Larry D. would ask, "Have you taken your medicine?" and I would go into a rage! What did he mean? Was I that bad? Yes, I was! To be 100% honest, I don't know how bad it was. With the amount of medication I was taking, a significant amount of my memory is distorted. I lost track of time for the first time in my life; I wasn't sure of anything.

My OCD tendencies went out of the window. My organizational skills disappeared. I would misplace items, forget to do tasks, and couldn't recall simple words. After gathering things before bed for L.J. to go to the babysitter, I wouldn't be able to find them the next morning. I would read a lesson to teach my students and then have to re-read it before presenting it. My doctor would listen to my frustrations and tell me that it would get better with time.

The symptoms for psychotic drugs are outrageous! I was impulsive, antisocial, loss of appetite, and struggled with erratic behavior. When I asked for a reduction in medication, he explained that it wasn't a good idea. He suggested since I would take them the rest of my life, I would adjust. As hard as it was to hear, I accepted it.

Late 2002 – 2003

This time frame of my life is not as defined, but still significant. I refer to this as "The Lost Year." My memory is usually impeccable with vivid descriptions, but not for roughly these 365 days. The amount of psychiatric treatment and the number of prescriptions made such an impact that I cannot recall much. Frankly, I was tiptoeing through life trying to survive. I was barely weighing 110 pounds. Sleep deprivation was my new normal due to insomnia.

There was still a smile on my face, but it was most certainly a fake one. Attending weekly therapy, I was continually digging into my past and sifting through the piles of dirt. Almost every session led me down a road to something else that I needed to deal with. The process was exhausting! I'm thankful my therapist was a Christian. He encouraged me to connect with the one thing that had always been a constant in my life, my faith.

It was easier said than done because when I thought about who had walked away, it almost broke me. I had been discussed behind my back, and it almost got to me. After receiving devastating news time and time again, I almost didn't recover. When disappointment came, I almost gave up. When I was hurt, I almost retaliated. Time after time, the devil almost had me right where he wanted me. BUT ALMOST DOESN'T .... COUNT! In my alone time, God began reminding me that I could be healed, free from people's opinions, victorious in every situation and an overcomer!

Time after time, the devil almost had me right where he wanted me. BUT ALMOST DOESN'T COUNT!

Although I lost a lot that year, I also regained my faith. Thankfully, I was beginning to feel alive again. God was restoring my joy and peace. The latter part of the summer of 2003,

I was finally acclimating to my medication. I was feeling more like myself and had regained control of a sense of normalcy. Unexpectedly, I had to stop taking the medication because I was expecting! Baby number two was coming, and we decided to have a "surprise" baby and not find out the gender.

2004

Joel 2:25 says, *"I will give you back what you lost in the years when swarms of locusts, cankerworms, caterpillars, and the palmerworms ate your crop."* My colorful memories are revived in early 2004 when I was near the end of my pregnancy. This pregnancy was nothing like the first. In fact, it was the exact opposite! I was never sick and gained a lot of weight. For the first time ever, I was well over 200 lbs. and happy about it. With the vast difference in the two pregnancies, we were certain we would have a girl. God had another plan.

After nearly three years in the closet, the baby bag with "Lance: God's Helper" was claimed by our second son. He was due on Valentine's Day, but was born one week early on February 7th. There was an initial disappointment because we desired to have a daughter, but it did not last long! L.J., our oldest child, was most definitely a Daddy's boy. Naturally, days after his birth, Lance officially became Mama's baby.

With a simple look, he had me wrapped around his finger! Even as a baby, Lance would lay his head on my shoulder and pat my back. I told one of my friends that God sent him to remind me that I was loved. That statement is not to slight my husband or our firstborn in any way! My love for both of them and how it came to be is special and unique as well. Lance is my sunshine after the storm baby. God allowed me to give him life when I was feeling lifeless.

During my six week check-up, precancerous cells were found on my cervix. The doctor explained the negative possibilities, and after discussion, we determined I would undergo a tubal ligation procedure. We made the decision because we felt our family was complete.

Lance was the perfect addition to our family! He was an extremely happy baby and smiled often. L.J. was a very helpful big brother and was quick to assist however and whenever he could. Everyone warned me about the changes that would occur with two children, and it became clear quickly. While L.J. was still difficult to put to bed every night, Lance would go to sleep quickly. When he would cry, we would make sure his needs were met and then put him back in his bed.

This was the second time around, and we were not only more experienced, but also smarter (we read even more parenting books). Caring for Lance was much less stressful because I had done it before. Of course, there were a few times that I questioned myself and whether I could handle mothering two children. Having a busy toddler and an infant was a lot of work, but Larry D. and I worked well together as a team. When Lance entered our family, he brought a sense of balance. More or less, we both took on the responsibility of providing the primary needs of one of the boys.

Life was full, and we were far extended, but it was working. I think we were so busy that I forgot about my bipolar diagnosis and the medication. When Lance was about three months old, the first negative emotion, low self-esteem, crept up on me. My entire life, I had worn a size 2-6. He was getting older, I had stopped breastfeeding and my "baby weight" was not falling off. As I purchased size 14-16 clothing, I was disgusted with myself.

After visiting my doctor, he suggested I get active. He explained this would help me lose the weight and could possibly help me avoid returning to mental-health medication. Both of those became my motivation. At my heaviest, I was 222 pounds. People don't believe it, but it's true! I will never forget seeing those numbers on the digital scale. Every morning, I would get up early and walk 4 miles at the track. I watched the clock at the bank across the street to make sure I had plenty of time to go home and get the boys to Head Start and the babysitter.

I continued this regiment for approximately six months and completely cut out all carbohydrates (mostly bread and potatoes). That sacrifice took a lot of commitment, but I knew for my life, marriage, and motherhood to continue on a good path, I had to do it. Larry D. never complained about my weight. I decided to diet and exercise because I knew I would not be able to live a happy life otherwise. As I was losing the weight, I began to feel better about myself! Re-establishing my sense of self made me feel brand new!

CHAPTER 13

Living Rejected

"Even if my father and mother abandon me, the Lord will hold me close."

— Psalm 27:10

After having my two sons, and being so madly in love with them, the thought of a person's natural parents abandoning their offspring is baffling. We literally owe our being to the individuals that God chose to be our father and mother. However, the scripture that David shares in Psalm 27:10 is proof that not all parents are capable of caring for their children. The story of Moses in Exodus 2:6-9 speaks of his parents forsaking him. God provided the king's daughter and a nurse, the child's own mother, to care for him.

Throughout this book, I have shared liberally about rejection. After many years of trying to figure out where this Spirit of Rejection entered my life, it finally became very clear that the absence of a relationship with my biological parents was the entryway. This chapter specifically uncovers the depth of my greatest battle and victory: Living Rejected.

Returning to a normal life after having our second child was much less difficult than I had anticipated. The 2004-2005 school year was the final year teaching at Northwest Elementary. I was the Math Instructional Resource Teacher (IRT). I spent my final two years working with teachers and students to increase knowledge in both literacy and math. This was an effort to prepare children (K-4) for state testing. That summer, my husband saw a job in the classified section of the newspaper and brought it to my attention.

The position was an Educational Manager with the local Head Start agency and would allow me the chance to work with teachers more. My love for teaching was still there; however, I had found my sweet spot: training and professionally developing other educators. I interviewed for the job and was given an offer the next day! The thought of a new adventure within the education field was extremely exciting. Learning about Families and Children Together, Inc. (F.A.C.T.) and the world of Early Childhood was a steep learning curve. A new work environment, co-workers, and the content were very overwhelming. With the help of a few kind people, I mastered things at a rapid rate. I began preparing to meet the staff who would be under my supervision.

Moments ago, I mentioned "a few kind people." That purposely alludes to the fact that there were others who were not. My time at Northwest was like a family-like atmosphere. I was not used to being uneasy and uncomfortable around colleagues. At first I thought it was because I was new, but even after the newness wore off, I faced hostility from a group of my co-workers. I was taunted, given the cold shoulder, challenged in meetings, and outright disrespected on multiple occasions. Three different times I was called a "Nigger." When I complained about the racial slur to the supervisor, I was told that I was being too sensitive and needed to work at resolving conflicts.

I had never had that problem before. From an early age, I had always made friends easily. The rejection by co-workers, vast amount of travel, and my workload led me back down the path to depression. At the end of the day, I would pick up the boys, feed and bathe them, stay in the shower as long as possible to drown out my weeping and go to bed. The feelings were familiar, and I decided to return to my therapist and was prescribed medicine again to help me cope.

At the same time, Larry D. and I were at odds a lot, and our marriage was in a slump. As I look back, we both could have worked on some things, but neglecting my mental wellness was at the top of the list. The symptoms of taking medication and focusing at work were nearly impossible. Through a lot of prayers, I was able to get organized, do my job effectively, and learned to ignore the naysayers. A couple of more times, I complained to management, however, there was no action taken. After one altercation, I was told that I needed to give people room "to have a bad day." I knew that everyone had bad days.

Nonetheless, whether we have been disappointed, hurt, lied to, gossiped about, misunderstood, abused, misused, or criticized, these occurrences should not be used as permission or excuses to treat others badly. With that said, a friend's reminder comes to mind, "Even when you're mad, you have to be saved." When work would become too much to bear, I would run to my safe haven, church. During this time, Larry D. and I were helping at his father's second church, Abundant Life (El Dorado). Every other Sunday, we would be in charge of the church services as his father and mother traveled to the church in Emerson.

We were dedicated to ministry in every way. Our attendance, service, and financial support were unwavering. Someone once said, "Tough times don't last, tough people do." When it came to ministry, we had both been hurt, but we were tough. His parents obviously had confidence in our ability, and we wanted nothing more than to please them and God. Since I was struggling with depression again, I found myself thinking about the following: What does God think of me? I worried that He was growing tired of my inconsistencies. I considered myself blessed, but wasn't sure I deserved the blessings.

One Sunday evening after church, I was called in the office by my Pastor and 1st Lady (my in-laws). He did the majority of the talking. With what felt like no warning, he told me it was time for me to be an Aspiring Missionary. This was a title given in the Church of God in Christ to women who would later earn an Evangelist Missionary license. Due to my inability to stand up to them and the fear of saying I didn't agree, I concurred.

Larry D. and I had been married five years. Living up to his parent's standard was not only his desire, but also mine. I had always conformed to gain their approval and did not want to disrespect them. I was desperately trying to avoid rejection. If I had told them no, it would have been considered blatant defiance. Therefore, shortly after that, I did my genesis message "More Than Meets the Eye." My honest assessment is that I was originally called by man, not by God. If I could go back, I would have said, "Not now."

When people call you, the devil is standing on the sidelines devising a plan to get you out of the game. He sends in his greatest defense to tackle you. It's only when you've had an inner call from God that you can be successful in ministry. Maybe my leaders didn't realize it, but I was in a very unstable state. On the surface, I looked okay, but I wasn't. Each time I would make progress, a detour, speed bump, dip, exit, stop sign, or road closed sign would appear. I had no idea it was preparing me for the next portion of my journey.

Not many months from that, my husband was ordained as an Elder. That meant he would soon be appointed to pastor a church. Finally, it all made sense! Suddenly, being a servant in the church wasn't enough. If he was potentially going to be a pastor, I needed to "come up" to that. Being named an Aspiring Missionary was only the beginning of the crash course in being a "Woman of God." In my therapy sessions, as my counselor and I would discuss my troubles at work and church, he would offer the following thoughts (I recorded them in my journal and read them daily): "Know yourself. Know you are where you are for a reason. You are worthy. Don't pretend to be what you are not because you are already more than you appear to be."

. . . .

"Know yourself. Know you are where you are for a reason. You are worthy. Don't pretend to be what you are not because you are already more than you appear to be."

. . . .

Those words helped me tremendously, both naturally and spiritually. I was tired of down-playing who I was (particularly at work) and who I knew God wanted me to be (in ministry). He had provided me with so many testimonies, helped me overcome so much, and forgiven me for even more. I wanted to stand tall and declare that I didn't need the approval of others, but at that time, I did not have the strength. 2 Corinthians 3:5 says, *"Not that we are competent in ourselves to claim anything, but our competence comes from God."* While I was being told what to wear (dresses and long skirts) and what not to wear (make-up, fingernail polish, and short hair), I was not competent enough to know that those things were not important in the eyes of God.

Whoever said, "Sticks and stones may break your bones, but words never hurt," was lying! Words wound! I want to encourage you to avoid allowing people to manipulate you into thinking that being like them is the only way to God. He is God all by Himself, and He does not need assistance. Around this same time, Larry D. had persuaded me to connect with my biological father, Charley Roy. The boys were small, so we visited Russellville once or twice a year so that he could see them. He and I would talk every few months.

Most times, when he called, he was intoxicated and would upset me. I wanted to have a relationship with him, but not like that. I asked my dad to call sober or not at all. That led to a long period of us not talking. I wasn't sure of where Marsheill was and only heard from her on my birthday and Christmas. She would usually send cards which I would read and throw away. My adoptive parents and I were on speaking terms, but conversations rarely happened. If I had not been so busy with my family, career, and church, I would have certainly buckled under the pressure.

To add to the pressure, in January of 2006, Larry D. was appointed to pastor. I was happy for him because he had been so faithful! At the same time, I was nervous and uncertain of what we were getting into. We went to the church, Louann Church of God in Christ, for the first time on a Friday night. Larry D. preached, and then we were called to the altar and prayed over. That was it! Two days later, we were Pastor Larry D. and 1st Lady P.J. There was no training, there wasn't a pep talk. No one even bothered to introduce us to the four members of the church.

We met them in Sunday School. We were brand new and young. The members were all old enough to be our parents or grandparents. And a few of them made sure we knew it. Immediately, Larry D. thrust himself into pastoring. I led the music worship and remained quiet unless someone spoke to me. His mother, who had been a pastor's wife for many years, had already given me instructions for my new role.

A few weeks in, I noticed the behavior of a couple of people. I wondered: how can one decide they don't like a person who they don't know? Easy! If a preconceived notion has already been established, the person in question is already at a disadvantage.

It's impossible to win over people who have decided (in their own ignorance) who you are and what you're about. One person, in particular, decided she did not like me. Things started with nasty looks and abrasive, sharp remarks and later escalated to threats.

After church one day, I had twelve missed calls and threatening voicemails. We were so shocked and unsure of what might happen that my husband and I decided to make a report to the police department. Through it all, my only desire was to be liked. I tried to earn the people's approval, but was not successful. I wore my hair the way I was told, I dressed in "church suits" with rhinestones, bling, and sequins and always had a smile, but that was not enough!

When I increased reading God's Word, I discovered that I also increased in love.

Take my advice, instead of working hard at getting people to like you, above all, be a person who is pleasing to God. It's not what people think, it's what God knows. In my husband's first year in Louann, I learned you can't expect more from people who need more Jesus. More Jesus means more love. Loving the unlovable is what he was teaching me. Until we can love like Him, we will not be able to move forward and truly minister to the needs of others.

L.O.V.E.

Listen (to your heart)

Overlook (faults)

Value (others)

Endure (the hard times).

That's LOVE! When I increased reading God's Word, I discovered that I also increased in love. It was then that I stopped taking my medication without the doctor's permission. I also stopped going to my therapy appointments. As time went on, we were so engulfed with ministry life that I became numb to everything else. If I could go back and tell my 29-year-old self one thing, it would be take care of yourself: physically, mentally, and emotionally. Church and religion caused me to lose sight of self. Authenticity was not popular in the church. Most people were hiding behind the "church face" mask; therefore, healing and growth were impossible.

I couldn't tell anyone about my struggles and what I was facing because I would be viewed as non-spiritual. Above all, I did not want to risk harming my husband's ministry. I had been told numerous times, "I was blessed to be a Yarbrough." At that time in my life, I wasn't sure how that made me feel, but it certainly wasn't good. It didn't feel like I was enough and that feeling in itself made me want to feel nothing at all! Consequently, under most circumstances, I chose not to.

Countless times I had to silence my flesh and speak the word of God.

When I did feel something, I felt alone and left out. Larry D. was doing all he could to carry the weight of being a husband, father, full time employee, and pastor. Unfortunately, that was at the expense of him not being able to balance those roles. I felt like I had been put aside and seemed invisible to the very people I wanted and needed in my life. Then it hit me, what if God was hiding me in plain sight? He comforted me and let me know that He was preserving and preparing me. Somewhere in the midst of this was His purpose for my life and ministry.

Countless times I had to silence my flesh and speak the Word of God. Proverbs 18:21 was a frequent reminder that life and death were in my tongue. Being a pastor's wife, I reduced the number of people who had enough access to my emotions to avoid being hurt. I learned that some people were sent into my life to keep me close to God. For the first couple of years, I convinced myself that something was wrong with me. Thankfully, I came to the knowledge that I was not the problem. I had slowly, but surely fallen right back into the deep pit of rejection and was dying spiritually.

In fact, a few years later, I was approached by a young lady who gave me a copy of a dream she had recorded in her journal. She had the dream in late 2007 or early 2008. Her pastor had instructed her not to contact me (because he did not want to alarm me and she did not know me on a personal level). In her writing, she referred to me as "Pastor Larry D. Yarbrough's wife" because she knew him from high school. It went on to say that I had died and she was attending my funeral. She said the church was filled to capacity and everyone was upset and crying.

During the sermon, a man with a bald head and dark complexion was preaching with great enthusiasm. She could not identify him, but said he preached so hard that I sat up in the casket, climbed out, and began to praise God and dance with all of my might! Incredibly, her dream had great significance and correctly depicted my status during that period of my life.

February of 2008, my husband and I were invited on a weekend get-away with another pastor, Alphonso Montgomery and his wife, Monique. Larry D. and Alphonso had been communicating since 2004 (on and off) and we had visited their church also. The first time we went to Led By the Spirit of God Church in Little Rock, the Lord used Monique to speak directly to my situation. We had visited Russellville one Friday and Saturday and decided to worship there on our way home. Through the Spirit of God, she was able to discern the mixed emotions that always followed visits to my biological family.

Other than that, I had only heard Alphonso preach a few times, but did not know either of them personally. Our ride to Dallas, Texas was quiet and a little awkward. There was a lot of small talk as we traveled, but after reaching our hotel and sitting down to eat, things changed. Monique smiled a lot, but didn't say much. Alphonso, on the other hand, was full of questions. As he asked more about us, we shared. Initially, we talked about our churches, jobs, and children. Somehow, as we continued to talk, we started going deeper. I had always been a little guarded about sharing details of my past but talking to them was easy.

It wasn't long before the complexity of my past triggered the passion in both of our new acquaintances. We talked for hours, but I recall two portions of the conversation as if it was yesterday. Monique asked me "Who are you?" I replied, "A wife, mother, career woman, etc." Her response was, "Those are your roles. Who are you?" Unfortunately, I couldn't answer with clarity. Alphonso asked question after question and later said to his wife, "Baby, she needs us to be her parents." She smiled and continued to listen as he began to talk about the role of Spiritual Parents. I was all ears, but very skeptical as he poured out his heart. I had just met them and frankly didn't trust them.

Additionally, I already had two sets of parents. Neither had worked out for me. I had no desire to subject myself to the pain and disappointment of that again. When we parted for the evening, I told Larry D. that I thought they were nice, but I didn't expect anything from them. He urged me to give them a chance and have a good time. The rest of the weekend was very enjoyable, and there were several life-changing thoughts shared. When this stranger (with a bald head and dark complexion-the man from the dream) and his wife spoke, my heart, mind, and spirit were awakened. I became a sponge absorbing every word they said and held on to them for dear life.

> **I learned that I couldn't hold other people hostage for the hurt that other's had inflicted on me.**

That weekend was a new beginning for me, and it affected every aspect of my life. I learned that I couldn't hold other people hostage for the hurt that other's had inflicted on me. The Montgomerys began to drill in me that every situation had happened for a reason. Pastor Al and Lady Monique earned my trust by being there for me through many tough times. She understood my struggles as a Pastor's wife. When I called her to vent, she didn't judge me or immediately accuse me of doing wrong.

Instead, she inquired about something that no one had ever mentioned to me before. She asked,

"Who Pastors the Pastor's Wife?" Those words resonated with me so deeply. I don't believe it was ever Larry D.'s intention to leave me uncovered while he was covering the sheep but it happened. Monique mothered me through so many instances. Her grace and wisdom gave me a fresh outlook. It wasn't long before she became my "Mama Monique." Right alongside her, Pastor Al was consistently my sounding board. He asked me to lay my burdens on him instead of Larry D. At the start, I did not fully understand. Now I realize he was able to relate to the untiring responsibility and load that my husband was under as a Pastor. Additionally, his offer to father me took that duty off of Larry D.

We had been married for eight years, and I had unconsciously wanted him to be both my husband and father. Daddy Al told me I was expecting too much from my husband. He was right. At the age of 29, at last, I was feeling accepted and approved by my God-given, Spiritual Parents.

What the enemy meant for evil, God meant for my good. I was no longer holding on to my past, but stretching toward my future. I had what I needed to build a bridge and get over it. It wasn't guaranteed to be easy, but I knew it would be worth it. If I didn't finally deal with it (rejection) it would forever deal with me. A friend once said, "Why do you want people in your life who aren't good for you?" She had a point. While I was longing for my biological and adoptive parents, time had proven that they were not good for me. One day, while in worship, God whispered, "They don't want you because you don't belong to them. You belong to me."

Those who deserted me never deserved me. They served their purpose. God used them for the season in which they were present. This revelation was a great benefit to me at work too! In spite of the recurring issues with my difficult co-workers, I had learned their opinions of me did not matter. God's favor had allowed me to build a rapport with the majority of the people I worked with and I had also gained a great deal of knowledge along the way.

That particular program year as the Arkansas Better Chance coordinator, I served in a dual role by also undertaking the job of an on-site Program Director. I continued to travel five counties (being the Education Manager for several classrooms) but spent the majority of my time in an administrative role, supervising the day-to-day operations of a preschool.

At the time, the Murmil Heights Preschool campus was a place of refuge for me. I had finally escaped the toxic environment that I had been subjected to for the past three years. The people who worked there were amazing, but they had rarely been told that. My primary goal was to appreciate, unite, and encourage the building personnel. I had watched from a distance and saw how their hard work was never enough. Within a matter of months, we were a strong staff and an even stronger family. My office assistant, all of the teaching staff, and even the custodian were performing at levels that were positively affecting the children's outcomes. In many ways, I became a shield for the unfair treatment that some of the Central Office Coordinators had once inflicted on the staff.

As their leader, I took the criticism and negative comments. Several days, I wanted to walk out, retaliate and treat people the way I was being treated, but I didn't. The devil's desire was for me to give up and quit. When reports that left my office "correct" were returned as "incorrect," I worked on them until the "powers that be" were satisfied. After I resubmitted them and they were accepted, I learned to make copies of my originals to beat them at their own game. I know that sounds awful and it was. Migraine headaches would plague me almost weekly (stress). But other than those setbacks, I was extremely happy working in the Early Childhood community. While in that role, I was introduced to one of my most favorite things to do, present professional development sessions at local, state, and national conferences.

Later in 2008, a few days before my 30th birthday, I began feeling sick. Excessive nausea, vomiting, and abdominal discomfort forced me to go to the OB-GYN (Obstetrician-Gynecologist). I'll never forget that day, September 9, 2008, my birthday! When I checked in, the receptionist asked why I came on my birthday. I explained I felt bad and couldn't go on like that another day. After the preliminary tests, the nurse entered the exam room and exclaimed, "Happy Birthday, you're pregnant!" My jaw dropped! I said, "Thanks, but that can't be possible because my tubes are tied." She smiled and said the doctor would be in shortly.

Moments later, he entered the room asking me over and over, "Are you in pain?" I told him there was no pain, but I felt awful. The information he shared revealed that my HCG levels showed that I was pregnant. He went on to explain that I was the "0.1%" because only about one in every two hundred women gets pregnant after a tubal ligation. The news was coming at me too fast. I called Larry

D. To say the least, he was shocked!

I told him to meet me at the hospital for an ultrasound. Before that, my doctor did a full Pap smear which is a routine for prenatal care. He told me he needed to check for cervical cancer since I had a history of precancerous cells. As I was headed to the hospital, they told me the biopsy results would be available in a couple of days.

Sitting in the waiting room, we were stunned. Both of us knew something was off, but being pregnant had never crossed our minds. As the tech placed the ultrasound gel on my stomach, the familiarity of the procedure charged my motherly instincts. As she moved the probe around, she asked us a few questions and then became silent. I asked if something was wrong and she said the baby was "hiding." She consulted with someone by phone and then said it would cause some discomfort, but she needed to do an internal ultrasound. I had a little pain during the procedure, but more importantly figured out there was a problem. After a long silence, she said she couldn't find anything. This time she left the room and told me to get dressed.

The nurse re-entered and said my doctor would contact me. That was a Tuesday because on Thursday, I went back to the doctor. The look on my physician's face was a sign that we weren't about to get good news. He delivered two diagnoses: an ectopic pregnancy (the baby was in my fallopian tubes) and the strong recommendation to have a hysterectomy. Following those two pieces of news, I was shattered and scared. I was informed that only about 1 in 50 babies survive an ectopic pregnancy. Additionally, he explained that the amount of precancerous cells that were on my cervix would more than likely result in full-blown cancer in a matter of 5-7 years.

Then he told me to report to the hospital at 6:00 AM the next morning. I said I wanted to get a second opinion. I knew whatever I decided would have to wait until Monday because my husband, family, and friends had planned me a 30th birthday party for the weekend. The doctor said he was fine as long as I wasn't in pain.

Friday, I had the results forwarded to Little Rock to my sister's gynecologist. The same day, I received confirmation that I needed to go through with the surgery (to remove the tubal pregnancy and have the full hysterectomy). After deciding I would have my 30th birthday party, I was told to report to the hospital at 6:00 AM, Monday morning. I called my supervisor in despair and told her I would be out for at least 6 weeks. It didn't take long for me to become fully aware of what was about to happen. On my birthday, when I realized I was pregnant, there was an immediate feeling of true happiness that flooded my heart and mind.

I cherished my role as a mother. With the reality of the pregnancy being unsuccessful and the major surgery I was about to undergo, I began to assimilate the seriousness of the matter. The pre-op evaluation required me to walk through the labor and delivery area of the Women's Center, and I lost it. I started crying and didn't think I would be able to stop. Why did this happen to me? Was I a bad mother? Did I do something to be punished by God?

I felt empty, guilty, angry, sad, shocked, and worthless. To be completely honest, out of nowhere, the devil spoke to my mind and told me this was "payback" for the abortion (from my college years). I was distressed and sorrowful, but could

For the first time ever, I felt rejected by God.

not find any relief as I prayed. For the first time ever, I felt rejected by God. I tried so hard to think on the Bible passage about how He would never leave me or forsake me, but I wasn't comforted by it. Thankfully, after reaching out to my Spiritual Parents, I was reminded of how God treats our sin (even my abortion), and I searched the scriptures.

Since that time, I've referenced these scriptures on numerous occasions when the devil tries to make me feel guilty:

- *God throws your sin into the sea.* (Micah 7:19)

- *God treads your sin underfoot.* (Micah 7:19)

- *God throws your sin behind His back.* (Isaiah 38:17)

- *God blots out your sin.* (Isaiah 43:25)

- *God forgets your sin.* (Hebrews 8:12)

- *God removes your sin.* (Psalm 103:12)

- *God covers your sin.* (Romans 4:7-8)

- *God washes your sin.* (Isaiah 1:18)

- *God cancels the debt of your sin.* (Colossians 2:14)

- *God forgives your sin.* (1 John 1:9)

Nothing can comfort us like the Word of God. I read the passages over and over until they desensitized my sadness. Validation from the scriptures gave me access to another point of view. What the devil was trying to make me believe was a lie. God showed me the truth!

My 30th birthday weekend, orchestrated by my husband and closest friends, was spectacular and frankly, exactly what I needed before embarking upon the next six weeks. The physical and spiritual pain of the surgery was tremendously draining! Like so many other things, this time of recovery and isolation crushed my spirit. My heart was broken too. Lying in bed, I opened my Bible to Psalm 34:17-18, *"The righteous cry out, and the Lord hears them; he delivers them from all their troubles. The Lord is close to the brokenhearted and saves those who are crushed in spirit."* I was struggling, and it was an agonizing feeling. I asked myself, "What am I doing here, again?"

With a strong recommendation from my husband and Spiritual Parents, I started taking my medication again and obeying the doctor's orders. My obedience was a sacrifice. I heard someone say that God takes good notes so we can't get weary in doing what's right because there is a reward! I was definitely rewarded at the end of taking the medication for two consecutive years. For the first time in eight years, I did not miss a single dose.

Once the meds were in my system again, I was able

to function without switching back and forth from allowing the devil to take control of my emotions and reactions. Before that, my angry fits would come out of nowhere, and that was not healthy for my marriage or family. When I took the medication faithfully, without wavering, I felt amazing. As I was doing as the doctor recommended, I noticed I was changing. I was ready to take back my life and no longer be controlled.

In the book *Shadow Boxing*, Dr. Henry Malone states, "It's impossible to belong to God and the devil at the same time. As a matter of fact, the devil doesn't want or need to own you as long as he can control you." It was my desire to only belong to God, but I also desired to be controlled by Him. I did not want to allow the devil to manipulate me into believing that God had abandoned me like my earthly parents.

In keeping with the theme of only belonging to God, I started to venture out in order to repair some relationships. When my adoptive parents called to ask me to take over the management of their finances, I was able to say yes. After many years of being estranged, I was finally ready to try and do what was right (honor them) even when it didn't feel good. I decided to try something different. I had to be willing to step out on faith and disregard what had happened throughout the years. This was huge! When we allow Him, God can and will restore. At first, I thought things were coming easier to me because of the medication. After a while, I refused to accept that. I knew without a doubt God was doing something new in me. God met me right where I was.

He was radically transforming my life! My relationship with Him was finally where it needed to be. I knew with God, my weaknesses would be covered by His strength. With Larry D.'s blessing, mid-November 2010, I asked for my doctor's permission to stop taking the prescriptions. My doctor agreed as long as I promised to let him know if I needed to return to the regiment. For two weeks, I reduced my dosage. On December 1, 2010, I did not take the pills. I was thinking clearly and felt as if I could conquer the world!

Now, almost eight years have passed, and I have never had to return to the medication! Contrary to the original diagnosis, I will not take medication for the rest of my life! God's grace and mercy have upheld me! Have I thought about returning to fill the prescriptions? Yes! People questioned my decision and even suggested that I keep the prescriptions filled. But when I made that decision, for the first time, I was able to truly deal with all of the raw emotions. I faced my abandonment issues and found they served a cause.

Abandoned

Abandoned, forsaken am I? Deserted and cast aside, why? Forgotten, discarded, it's all the same. While I'm feeling empty, they don't seem to know my name. Given up and neglected, left out in the cold. These heavy emotions soon grow old. Jilted like a bride with no groom – yes, the accuser of the brother sought to bring me nothing, but gloom. I guess he didn't know I would be adopted and made a royal heir. There's enough for me, and I have plenty to share! My Father chose to take me as His own. To me, unmerited love has He shown. Mercy and grace He gives freely each day. After all I've been through to get to this place. I wouldn't trade my journey. I will finish this race!

With the absence of the mental-health medications, I continued therapy (this time marriage counseling included) to aid in my healing process. The Fall of that year, I started attending classes to become licensed as an Evangelist Missionary in the Church of God in Christ (COGIC).

The classes were designed to equip me with the knowledge needed to evangelize and enhance the work of my local church.

I was recommended by my pastor (Larry D.), approved by a District Superintendent, and accepted by the Supervisor of Women on the state level. The license, which I earned in January 2009, was not something I necessarily wanted, but more so what I needed. The consecration ceremony involved me taking a pledge and served as public affirmation. Unfortunately, that did not translate to the private.

Put plainly, church people were still mean. I was different (mostly because I was young), and I was treated as such. I wore shorter hair than most women, and my dresses were rarely floor-length. Sometimes I wore stockings and sometimes I didn't. I was a "1st Lady," but I talked to everyone, and I was an exuberant "Praiser." I believe in praising God freely, in dance and with my voice! But I was told Godly women should be quiet: seen, not heard.

My nature had always been lively, vivacious, and sociable. Needless to say, I was not afforded many opportunities to minister in COGIC churches because everything about me went against the grain. I've mentioned it previously, but I must restate that I cannot adequately express the emotional pain of rejection from Christians, people of God. Speaking of people of God, in addition to experiencing repudiation from my family of origin, co-workers, and life in general, facing resistance from my in-laws added to the pain.

From the inception of my relationship with Larry D., their goal seemed to be to change me, make me what they perceived as better, and to create someone more fitting for their son and family. Going back to the late 90s, I longed for people to accept me as I was – imperfect. Honestly, during those years, I thought so lowly of myself that I felt privileged to be in a relationship with my Pastor's son. As time progressed, they consistently chose to push me away instead of embracing me.

I'll be the first to repeat that I was (and am) far from perfect, but I can also say everything I did in the early years was to gain their approval. No matter how hard I tried, their actions and words were always a reflection of how I didn't measure up to their standard. Honestly, I was okay as long as I followed instructions, but as soon as the intelligent, self-assured young lady would surface, I was doing too much. Initially, I was referenced as their "daughter in law," but shortly after the newness wore off, I became the "son's wife" and later the "mother of their grandchildren." The latter of the two still baffle me! For years, I've wondered how can anyone be so deeply and affectionately in love with my two sons, but not accept their mother?

After eleven years of going through those things (secretly), a family meeting was held, and everyone broke their silence. The "pink elephant" that had been in the midst for years was most definitely visible! An avalanche of hurt feelings, misunderstandings, accusations and negative opinions filled the room, and the majority of it was towards me and Larry D. I'm sure everyone was shaken; however, my soul was absolutely disturbed to the core. After walking out that night, I was almost certain everything that had transpired would throw me back into a dark place.

A couple of days later, additional accusations came that I thought would end our marriage. But like a sermon I once delivered, "It Had to Happen!" That entire situation was a test! Everything that happened was supposed to be the last straw. It was intended to break me, and it almost did.

As a matter of fact, the days following that meeting were so difficult that I was very close to having my mental health medication refilled. But God was gracious enough to keep me. I felt like my heart had been ripped out, again. The difference this time was that the pain was not only mine but also my husband's and unfortunately, it eventually affected our sons as well.

Three short months later, my adoptive mother, Ernestine, fell ill and never recovered. In her hospital room, while we were alone, I talked to her. Some days, I think back and pray she was able to both hear and understand. Firstly, I asked her to forgive me for anything I had done to cause the years of estrangement between us. I also told her I loved, appreciated, and forgave her. She passed away the next day, and my heart was at peace. The end of 2011 was extremely challenging!

As I was trying to get through it and over it (rejection), I began to study and read everything I could. One piece of research spoke of scientists placing individuals in functional MRI machines. After doing so, they would tell the people to think about a recent rejection. What they concluded was shocking. The human brain becomes activated in the same areas when we feel rejection as when we experience physical pain. That certainly explains why even the smallest refusals, denials, and lack of acceptance hurt more than they should.

Rejection provokes and produces literal (albeit,

emotional) pain. In fact, it comes directly from the devil and is a malicious attempt to take our love, joy, and peace. Even though the devil wants us to live in complete devastation, desolation, and destruction, God is able to heal and restore! Through God's divine power, I have taken the theme scripture of this chapter and applied it to my life.

The Lord has most certainly "held me close." It is in Him that I live, move, and have my being (Acts 17:28). Without Him, I am rejected, but with Him, I am accepted.

One of my husband's favorite sayings is, "Rejection is God's protection." When you feel rejected, don't give up too soon. Hang in there. No matter what the devil tries to tell you, choose to agree with God!

CHAPTER 14

Agreeing with God

"Consider it pure joy, my brothers and sisters, whenever you face trials of many kinds, because you know that the testing of your faith produces perseverance. Let perseverance finish its work so that you may be mature and complete, not lacking anything."

— *James 1: 2-4*

Why do bad things happen to good people? How can one be born a statistic, life rejected, and agree with God? The solution is easy: in the words of an old song, *"Accept What God Allows."* The Creator, God, is omnipotent, omnipresent, and omniscient. He's sovereign. His matchless and supreme authority assures us that when He does something, He knows exactly what, why, and how He wants it done.

God does not have to share His reasons for making decisions. Our full confidence must be in His ability to orchestrate every detail of our lives single-handedly. I first came to this revelation on the road trip to Texas (2008) with our Spiritual Parents. I will never forget Daddy Al looking at me in the rearview mirror and saying, "Shaneil, you need to agree with God."

In that weekend, I had opened my heart and told them about a lot of my sufferings and losses in life. My experiences of hardship, disappointment, and grief had produced years of frustration, hurt, and even illness. I had no idea that I had further complicated many of the situations because I didn't accept what God had allowed and moved on. The saying is true: life goes on. No matter how tragic the situation or terrible the circumstance, when God has spoken - sometimes by words, actions, or no response, it's time to go forward!

I'm sure you've heard the phrase, "He either says yes, no, or wait." Regardless of God's answer, we must trust Him. While celebrating the New Year in January of 2017, it was brought to my attention that if I was still dealing with things from the past year (or further back), I wouldn't really have a "New Year." Those words stuck with me and I decided to pray and seek God for how to go forward and leave the past behind me. At that time, He led me to the story of the man at the Pool of Bethesda (John 5). I had read or heard the story many times. That particular time, I was able to relate to it differently.

The words seemed to jump off the page and speak to me. The man in the story was 38. I was 38. He had been lying by the pool for all of those years, and I too had been "lying" in the same state for far too long. Time and time again, God had asked me, "Do you want to be healed?" Like the man, I had made excuse after excuse to explain the tardiness of moving into my place of healing.

I had been in and around the church my entire life. After accepting salvation at an early age, sadly, I had forfeited the true blessing of the cross: full deliverance and freedom from adversity! With this new outlook, I prepared a message titled, "Now or Never." I knew as I shared with the people of God that Sunday morning, I was actually talking to myself! Shortly after, I went through a box, which was packed away, to find a notebook that was given to me during the first Christian Women's Conference I ever attended.

After accepting salvation at an early age, sadly, I had forfeited the true blessing of the cross; full deliverance and freedom from adversity!

The hostess, Pastor Reece Broadnax, had conducted a special session for Pastors' wives. While in the gathering, she encouraged and prayed for us. With our eyes closed, she said, "A few of you have a story, a book, and it must be written for others to read." She went on to say she would be placing a notebook in front of the ones who God had revealed to her through prayer. When I opened my eyes, the notebook was there. I was fearful, but I knew she was Spirit led. My only regret is that it took me nearly nine full years to truly understand the need for this book.

Over the years, as I wrote little by little, situations would arise, and I would stop. I wondered if my husband and children would be embarrassed, if my family would be upset, if people in the church would judge me, and if my colleagues would lose respect for me. Finally, I reached the point that I trusted God. When those doubts surface, I refer to the scripture: Psalm 56:3-4 which says, *"When I am afraid, I will trust in you. In God, whose word I praise, in God I trust; I will not be afraid. What can mortal man do to me?"*

Once I decided to "Agree with God," things became so much clearer. Alas, I was able to recognize His hand over my life. As I bring this portion of my life story to an end, I will provide a few examples of how I "Agree with God."

A Once In a Lifetime Chance

Throughout my life, my feelings towards my biological mother, Marsheill, had always been conflicted. Similarly, I didn't have many positive emotions towards my biological father, Charley Roy. The difference between the two was that I rarely knew where she was located. Once I found him, all I had to do was call and ask if we could visit.

Larry D., the boys, and I looked forward to our trips to Russellville to see my Dad Roy, my grandmother, and the Nichols family. They were always kind, welcoming, and opened their hearts and homes to us with gladness. Easter weekend of 2012, we decided to visit them. We were there for a couple of hours when someone mentioned that my mother was also in town.

Before I knew it, my mother was walking into the yard. My father and I were on the porch, and she joined us. Crazy enough, I was 33 years old and for the first time ever had both of my parents in the same place at the same time! After the initial small talk, I began to ask questions about how they met and how I came to be. They talked about how over the years, Marsheill had been in and out of town. Each time she returned, they would pick up like old friends.

Then they told me "the story." Simultaneously, they completed each other's sentences. Dad Roy said she had "been with a couple of his friends" and knew she had "a lot going on," but he always helped her out. When she showed up late one night, he invited her to stay over. She agreed that she knew he would "take care of her." They explained how one thing led to another (I really didn't want details): the next morning he "cooked her breakfast" and she left.

My mother then said, "Shaneil, you were not conceived in love." I didn't hear much more after that statement. I was humiliated. Was that what I was worth: a friends with benefits encounter and breakfast? A few years later when I was asking for more clarity, she told me I was "a mishap." I wallowed in her words. What I had wanted my entire life, both of my parents, was actually too much to bear! This was a moment that ended up as a perfect representation of how we must agree with God. Neither of my biological parents was capable of parenting me. They couldn't give me what they didn't have. Her reputation of promiscuity and his alcoholism as well as dealing with PTSD following the Vietnam War made it impossible.

After that once in a lifetime opportunity, I had to force myself to see the positive in all situations. Sometimes we have to **G.R.O.W.U.P.**: "**G**et **R**id **of W**ho or **W**hat **U**psets **P**rogress!"

This is the only avenue to personal maturity and recognizing God's perfect plan. Hindsight really is 20-20. I didn't literally "get rid of" my biological parents, but I decided to let go of the pain. For years, I struggled with low self-esteem and shame because of who my parents were. I knew of my mother's poor reputation and my father's battle with mental health illness.

The devil was certainly on his job, always reminding me of where I came from. A friend once told me, "Every thought you have is not yours. Don't take ownership." That was one piece of advice that I still apply often. Another quote I love is from Pastor Joel Osteen, "You did not come from your mother, you came through your mother, from God." When my mother's words, "You were not conceived in love," come to mind, I am able to cast that down. God loved me enough to allow me to be born! My brokenness has turned into a blessing. My misery has become my ministry! God will get the glory out of my life!

The one time I sat and talked with my parents made it easier for me to love them. I have rarely heard from Marsheill since that weekend. Throughout the years, she has lived with a couple of my sisters and still stays in touch with them to some degree.

As for a relationship with me, she has surfaced here and there, but never stayed around for long. Our youngest son, Lance, fell in love with her, mostly because of our strong resemblance. I've heard many times I am her twin, and honestly, it's hard to hear, but true.

When my sons began to feel the pain of her disappearing acts, I knew something would have to change. They wanted to know when "Grandma Marsheill" would return and I couldn't answer. The few times she has contacted me did not end well. In recent years, I told her she no longer has permission to come in and out of my life and hurt me. She has the choice to either have a relationship or not. It's a difficult reality to face, but in this season, she has other priorities that don't include me.

One year after having them together, Dad Roy became ill and passed away. In the days leading up to his death, I drove to Little Rock every other day to sit with him and thoroughly enjoyed our father-daughter time. He wasn't usually very talkative, but for the period of those visits, he was. I believe he knew our time was limited. One of our last times together, Larry D. and I had the amazing opportunity to offer my father Christ.

Praise God, he accepted! The final time I stood by his bedside, everyone in the room could sense him transitioning to heaven. That same day, a couple of family members told me Dad Roy had "always known" I was his daughter. They shared that they knew also.

Of course this information created a lot of questions in my heart and mind, however, I chose to cherish the last few moments I had with him.

My love and appreciation for the short ten years I knew him are unexplainable. The relationships I've continued to cultivate with my Nichols family are a beautiful reminder of him. I won't pretend to understand everything concerning the relationship with my biological parents (or the lack thereof), but I agree with God.

Confessions of a
Motherless/Fatherless Child: If I Knew

If I knew your heart's beat, I would lie on your chest to listen to its rhythm. If I knew the strength of your arms, I would embrace you as tight as possible. If I knew the color of your eyes, I would look into them with love. If I knew your favorite flower, I'd pick them fresh from a garden. If I knew your phone number, I would call just to hear your voice. If I knew what you like to eat, I would invite you to dinner. If I knew your song of choice, I would sing the melody. If I knew you would read this, I would continue writing. Only, if I knew. – Shaneil

Purpose Served

My prayer is that as people read this book, they will realize my only motive is for God to get the glory. As I've written and re-read my accounts of situations, issues, and dilemmas, I can only stand in my truth. I cannot and will not attempt to tell anyone's story except for mine. I fully understand and respect that my biological sisters may have a completely different point of view concerning our adoptive parents. My ultimate goal has been to tell my story – no one else's.

I also don't intend to bring any dishonor to anyone. Making that statement is a great segue to explain the peace I have acquired concerning my adoptive parents. The sacrifice that Andrew and Ernestine Curley made is one that I will forever hold as one of my greatest blessings! When I think of where I could have ended up, I am so grateful that God used them to intervene. Life in their home was not perfect, but I have full confidence that they served their purpose. My mother, Ernestine, is gone to be with the Lord, however, her labor of love continues. She may not have done things the way I thought she should have, but God used her to provide me with an example.

Through her agreement with God to do the unthinkable (adopt 4 girls), she created a legacy that makes taking care of my children a priority. Likewise, my father, Andrew, was her partner in fulfilling the commitment that was put before them. Now that I'm a parent, I know the pressure was immense, but he stuck in there. In fact, I don't think he understood the purposefulness of his duty. Actually, adopting us was not only their decision but also a God-given assignment!

Present day, my Dad and I are able to communicate respectfully. Though we don't have a close-knit relationship, I strive to do as the Bible commands and show him "honor". Unfortunately, the strong bond I desired to have with my adoptive parents never came to fruition. We had some good times, but my truth is that they were fewer than our years of estrangement. In spite of that fact, when they asked me to handle their business several years ago, I did it with no hesitation. It was a huge undertaking with my busy life. Was it easy? No. But it was another effort to agree with God.

Many times, concurring with God's plan means tolerating His procedure to become His product. At first, I was not able to do good towards them under my own strength. Showing kindness to people I loved, who had not always shown me love, was a huge obstacle. In order to succeed, I needed God's Spirit. Zechariah 4:6 says, *"...you won't succeed by might or by power, but by my Spirit, says the Lord."*

I've previously mentioned the importance of accepting God's plan. I'll further state that His plan does not only consist of pleasant things. As a matter of fact, the good, the bad, and the ugly are all necessary. According to 1 Timothy 6:15, *"God... is the blessed controller of all things, the king over all kings and the master of all masters."* Even when we don't understand why, God is making all things work together (Romans 8:28). One of my therapists used a phrase that complimented this scripture, "They didn't stop anything."

Each time I would share how hurt I was about my adoptive parents' absence from my life, he would say, "They didn't stop anything." I knew he was right, but it took me years to truly acknowledge what God was using him to convey. When I stepped back and saw the big picture, I found comfort in what God had allowed.

He allowed me to feel isolated, abandoned, and unloved by my parents in order to teach me to rely on Him, not people. As a result, I'm conscious of the fact that if people aren't there, God doesn't want them there. While in most cases parents are there to assist their children with life's circumstances, God has taught me to pursue Him. In the words of another friend, "I use to go to my Daddy (or Mama)... until I got a relationship with the Father." My deep connection with God via worship, the Word, and living in His will makes it easier to agree with Him.

The Stamp of Approval

During the course of my life, rejection from family, friends, co-workers, and even strangers has left an undeniable impact. It might not be an official condition, but I like to say I suffered from "Approval Addition;" the need to be accepted and liked.

For years, I told people what they wanted to hear, tried to be someone they would find impressive, worried incessantly about what people thought of me, and feared criticism. Holding myself back, I negatively impacted my personal performance because of my desire to have people approve, like, accept, and love me.

This did not work well for me! Thankfully, I now find comfort in knowing that God approves of me. While He knows me and everything about me, including my flaws, He accepts and loves me! I have God's Stamp of Approval! Much like a product comes off the assembly line and receives a stamp of authenticity, we are God's masterpieces! We are not copies but originals crafted by the creator and it doesn't matter what people think!

In reality, what people know and what they think can be two very different things. One might think a person has it made and that they have it easy. However, what they don't know is how God's grace and mercy have helped that person to endure many difficulties. Another may think a person has received favors from people, but instead, that person is favored by God. People many times think they can take credit for a person's success, but God gets all of the glory! Lastly, it may appear that everyone is in competition, but actually, some people are simply confident in who God has made them to be. All of this is available when we choose to agree with God!

This is Where I Am

In the last thirteen chapters, I've shared from my heart. Trust me, I don't look like what I've been through! I've told where I've been. This is where I am now. Many things I said I would take to my grave are now fully exposed. Once I realized my past did not define me, I felt compelled to make sure others knew the same. Just like my past, my present and my future are completely in God's hands. Like the scripture that I mentioned at the beginning of this chapter states, I count it all joy! The very things that could have, should have, and would have taken me out have made me who I am today!

> **The very things that could have, should have, and would have taken me out have made me who I am today!**

Sharing God's word.

Interestingly enough, after studying the effects of not properly dealing with adversities, the weight of unsettled emotions manifested in my life in some ways. One of those has been the Spirit of Infirmity. Chronic asthma, cancer, mental illness, lupus, severe migraines, and even digestive problems are rooted in unforgiveness and operating in pity.

I'm grateful for Jehovah Rapha, the Lord our Healer. He is the great physician. All the years I refused to let go, I was miserable and refused deliverance. Today, I am healed and restored of all diseases. Another burden I carried for years was guilt and shame. The devil tricked me into thinking that I was damaged goods. He plagued my mind with years of hurt, anger, and fear.

The theme scripture of Changing Lives Ministries, my church home, is 2 Corinthians 5:17, *"Therefore if any man be in Christ, he is a new creature: old things are passed away; behold, all things are become new."* It's hard to admit, but even though I received salvation as a child, I did not fully accept full deliverance until I was in my mid-thirties! I am extremely thankful that I am new and I have a new outlook. In my current work as an Executive Director and Administrator of a group foster home, Agape House Children's Home, life has come full circle.

Each day, I look upon the faces of children who are literally where I came from. As I search for ways to positively impact their lives, I fully understand why I went through all of the things I've endured. I do what I can to keep myself on track and avoid returning to the dark places.

Here are a few of my favorite daily reminders:

"Nobody can hurt me without my permission."
– Mohandas Gandhi

"Never again will I justify the scars just because I love the person holding the knife."
– Steve Marbaoli

"Be who you needed when you were younger."
- Anonymous

"If you can't grow with me, you can't go with me."
– Sarah Jakes Roberts

"My experiences allowed me to have empathy
for people born unwanted. The very idea of
coming into the world wanted is a gift."
– Oprah Winfrey

"Don't give up on the new you,
the destiny you, the new creation you,
the powerful you, the intelligent you,
the purposeful you, the gifted you!"
– Alphonso Montgomery, D. Div.

"Rejection by people is a divine announcement
[from God] that they no longer have the capacity
to contain your greatness or support your
purpose and your destiny!"
– Dr. Cindy Trimm

"Don't become who hurt you."
– Anonymous

"This is my life... my story... my book.
I will no longer let anyone else write it:
nor will I apologize for the edits I make."
– Steve Maraboli

Above all things, I submerge myself in the Word of God (the scriptures at the beginning of each chapter are my go-to affirmations) and do all I can to strengthen my relationship with Him. I wholeheartedly embrace every moment that I'm blessed to have with my husband and two sons. When referencing them on social media, I use the hashtag, #My3Men. I'm immensely grateful for the opportunity to enjoy life with them. My small but strong circle which consists of my Covenant family, church family, members of my family of origin, dear friends, and colleagues all give me more than I will ever be able to repay them.

Today, I focus on what I have, not what I don't have. I focus my energy on my blessings, not my bruises. I choose to concentrate on the sunshine instead of the storms. I aim to keep my faith when fear arises. When we offer ourselves openly, God will always answer.

As Christians, when we make ourselves available, God can work in our lives. My prayer is that my testimony will be a blessing to many. As a wife, mother, Pastor's wife, friend, family member, community member, and a citizen of the Kingdom of God, I want to be an illustration of how we all have accessibility to resilience, transformation, God's grace, and unmerited favor. God's immeasurable love has superseded statistical data, my personal battle with rejection, and my hesitation to trust His divine plan.

. . . .

God's immeasurable love has superseded statistical data, my personal battle with rejection, and my hesitation to trust His divine plan.

. . . .

While many have buckled under the reality of their experiences, I have not only survived, but thrived. Every betrayal, heartache, and struggle that I thought was destroying me was actually shaping me. My life has turned out to be beautiful chaos. I'm in awe of how God has allowed me to overcome obstacles, find forgiveness, and discover my destiny. With reference to my destiny, as a gift, my Covenant brother, Prophet Kaderick and his wife, Debra Jones, shared with me the prophetic meaning of my name, Shaneil. Although for years, I preferred not to be called by my birth name, I now understand who I am:

Shaneil: Wise Champion & Advisor

You were created to speak wisdom into the lives of many. This wisdom, however, will only be gained through your ability to overcome great adversity. Just as Satan desired Simon Peter, to sift him as wheat, so does he desire you. But you need not ever be afraid for the Lord determined in eternity that you will always be a Champion. At the end of every victory, you will be called to strengthen others through the wise counsel you have gained from your victory!

Maybe you're like me, **Born a Statistic**. It's even quite possible you are **Living Rejected**. I plead with you to **Agree with God**. Open up to yourself. Be transparent with God.

If necessary, seek out help. He will make you better than you have ever been. When it's all said and done, God wants all of His people to live in abundance and victory!

The Yarbrough Family

Lance, Shaneil, Larry D., and L.J. (2018)

Made in the USA
Columbia, SC
19 September 2018